Etouffée, Mon Amour

Etouffée, Mon Amour

The Great
RESTAURANTS
of New Orleans

Photography and text by

Kerri McCaffety

Foreword by Peggy Scott Laborde

PELICAN PUBLISHING COMPANY
Gretna 2002

*The word "Pelican" and the depiction of a pelican are trademarks
of Pelican Publishing Company, Inc., and are registered
in the U.S. Patent and Trademark Office.*

Library of Congress Cataloging-in-Publication Data

McCaffety, Kerri.
 Etouffée, mon amour : the great restaurants of New Orleans / photography and text by Kerri McCaffety ; foreword by Peggy Scott Laborde.
    p. cm.
Includes bibliographical references and index.
 ISBN 1-56554-926-0 (alk. paper)
1. Restaurants—Louisiana—New Orleans—Pictorial works. I. Title.
TX945 .M485 2002
647.95763—dc21

2002005673

Front jacket: *Antoine's*
Back jacket: *Casamento's*
Page 1: *St. Roch Seafood*
Page 2: *NOLA*
Page 3: *Tujague's*
Page 4: *Bozo's—stained glass created by Ken Attenhofer*

Printed in Hong Kong

Published by Pelican Publishing Company, Inc.
1000 Burmaster Street, Gretna, Louisiana 70053

CONTENTS

Lost Restaurants 6

Preface 8

Introduction 10

New Orleans' Oldest Restaurants

Antoine's 19
Tujague's 30
Bruning's 36
Café Du Monde Coffee Stand 38

Late Nineteenth Century

Morning Call Coffee Stand 40
Commander's Palace 42
Emeril's Delmonico 48
Café Sbisa 53

Early Twentieth Century

Galatoire's 56
Acme Oyster House 60
Arnaud's 62
Broussard's 72
The Court of Two Sisters 78

Mangia Italiano

Brocato's 82
Central Grocery 85
Napoleon House 85
Fiorella's 86
Pascal's Manale 88
Casamento's 92
Domilise's 94
Mandina's 96
Charlie's Steak House 98
Liuzza's Lounge and Grill 99

The Croatian Kitchen

Mandich 101
Uglesich's 104
Ruth's Chris Steak House 107
Bozo's 108
Crescent City Steak House 110

Into the Swing Era

Mother's 112
Hansen's Sno-Bliz 113
Dooky Chase's 114

Franky and Johnny's 118
Gumbo Shop 122
Mosca's 125
Camellia Grill 128
Liuzza's Restaurant and Bar 130

The Birth of a Dining Dynasty

Brennan's 133
Mr. B's Bistro 140
Bacco 142
Red Fish Grill 144
Palace Café 146

Fifties and Sixties

Venezia 148
Rocky and Carlo's 149
Rib Room 150
Sid-Mar's 152
Jacques-Imo's 155
Zachary's 155

Creole in the Last Thirty Years

K-Paul's Louisiana Kitchen 157
Brigtsen's 158
Gabrielle 159
Emeril's 160
NOLA 161
The Bistro at Maison de Ville 163
Bayona 164
Peristyle 167
Christian's 171
Feelings Cafe 172
Jack Dempsey's 173
Gautreau's 174
Clancy's 176
La Crêpe Nanou 180
Upperline 183

The Modern Italians

Andrea's 185
Irene's Cuisine 186
Tony Angello's 186

A World Beyond Creole 188

Bibliography 190

Index 192

LOST RESTAURANTS

A Polynesian paradise, a slice of old Bavaria in downtown New Orleans, a menu that featured wild game way before there was an endangered species list—just a few tastes of some restaurants that exist now only in the city's memory.

Courtesy of Harry Batt, Jr.

A Taste of the Tropics and a Bit of Bavaria

On the south shore of Lake Pontchartrain was a restaurant with the feel of the South Pacific. Festooned with giant tortoise shells and fishnets, the Bali Hai was located within Pontchartrain Beach Amusement Park. Growing out of the late 1950s and America's fascination with Polynesia, and underscored by the resounding popularity of the novel turned musical, *South Pacific,* dinner at the Bali Hai was a culinary adventure. Tiki bowls, filled with rum and fruit juices, created some indelible memories for patrons.

Courtesy of Harry Batt, Jr.

So did Kolb's Restaurant. At the turn of the last century, Conrad Kolb created a Bavarian fantasy that included walls lined with beer steins and pictures of the old country. In later years, Kolb's became one of the first restaurants to feature crawfish dishes on the menu, in addition to the expected wiener schnitzel. Creole selections were offered alongside Teutonic fare at this landmark restaurant located in the business district, a half-block off of Canal Street. "Ludwig" was the moniker given to the lederhosen-clad mechanical figure that could be seen in the rafters, cranking an intricate belt system connected to ceiling fans. The fan operation was a remnant of the 1884 Louisiana Cotton Exposition, a world's fair. In later years, even after air conditioning became commonplace, Ludwig still turned the fans, continuing to fascinate not only kids but also the mostly adult male downtown clientele.

There was a touch of Spain in the décor of one of the local Morrison's cafeterias. "It had stars in the ceiling and Spanish tiles on the floor. You felt like you were in a Spanish hacienda, someone's villa. You dressed to go to Morrison's," remembered film critic Rex Reed, who, with his family, visited New Orleans often. Other cafeterias included Holsum, also downtown, and citywide, there were the A & G's. Music was on the menu at many of the A & G cafeterias, where organist Ray McNamara performed for patrons.

Call of the Wild

Hunting for wild game or for your first lobster? T. Pittari's was where the search ended and the meal began. According to Tom Pittari, Jr., in 1952 his dad brought the first lobster tank to New Orleans. "People had never seen a big crawfish before. We would serve between two and five thousand pounds of lobster per month," recalled Pittari. "Our specialty was Lobster Kadobster. My father came up with the name, kind of rhymed. We actually had the name copyrighted." The Kadobster concoction was a mixture of six different types of seafood artfully arranged in a lobster shell.

After lobster, at T. Pittari's, wild game was the big attraction. "We brought in tiger and water buffalo, hippopotamus, elephant, and of course, as we went along some of these items slipped off the menu because they really weren't quite palatable. But they were different and people wanted to try them," noted Pittari.

Courtesy of Tom Pittari, Jr.

Smoochin' and Munchin'

The Rockery Inn and Lenfant's were both well known for not only what took place inside the restaurants, but also what went on in the parking lot. Both had drive-up service. Waiters, called car hops, took care of orders. Rockery owner Vincent Signorelli recalled with a broad smile, "Some of the old car hops had different nicknames. Al Gaudet, we called him the 'Whistler.' He'd whistle when he was coming to bring the order, to warn people to get out of their 'wrestling hold' because he was coming to the car. I say 'wrestling hold.' Being cuddly. That's a nice way to put it."

Fine Dining under the Bridge

LaRuth's was located on the West Bank in Gretna, in an old shotgun-style home practically under the Mississippi River bridge. The restaurant was considered to be one of the leading dining establishments of its day. Chef Warren LeRuth, according to restaurant critic Tom Fitzmorris, combined cooking traditions directly from France with local restaurant techniques.

Courtesy of Tom Pittari, Jr.

Crabmeat St. Francis, LeRuth's own take on the classic Crabmeat Imperial dish, and oyster artichoke soup were his best-known dishes. He is also credited with developing Green Goddess salad dressing, which is now marketed by Kraft Foods. As a food consultant, LeRuth went on to develop the legendary red-beans-and-rice recipe for the Popeye's Famous Fried Chicken chain.

Beans That Counted

Buster Holmes' restaurant also served red beans and rice. The place's laid-back atmosphere, along with Holmes' warm personality, made for a winning combination. Holmes was known for feeding hungry patrons who couldn't afford the already-inexpensive check.

Eddie's and Chez Heléne were also known for their fine renditions of Creole soul food. Though gone, Chez Heléne was immortalized by the CBS television series *Frank's Place*. Today, Chez Heléne's chef, Austin Leslie, spices up the kitchen at Jacques-Imo's, and Eddie's son, Wayne Baquet, continues the family tradition at Zachary's restaurant.

The list of lost restaurants is, alas, a long one, but let us at least recall the gentility of Corinne Dunbar's, the art-deco glitz of Jonathan, along with West End restaurants such as Fitzgerald's and Maggie and Smitty's. The dining history of New Orleans is like a fine meal, made flavorful by great influences and ingredients.

Here's hoping that there are many more servings yet.

—PEGGY SCOTT LABORDE

PREFACE

Walker Percy wrote an essay called "New Orleans, Mon Amour" in 1968 in which he posited that the city would go to hell in the next few years. The only thing that might save it was "a certain persisting non-malevolence" resulting from years of cultural and ethnic blending. Either way, Percy said, New Orleans would never become "the likes of Dallas or Grosse Point."

Twenty-five years later, we have not descended into hell, and New Orleans is a long way from becoming like any other American city. And the cultural blending that inspired the indigenous attitude that Percy saw as our sole salvation continues to stimulate spiritual, musical, and culinary alchemy.

In a city where food is not just a passion but an obsession, where it is more than sustenance, where it is spiritual inspiration, where there are two times of day—mealtime and in between—restaurants are sacred institutions. They symbolize our oldest enduring traditions, act as settings for personal and cultural events, and contain the souls of families who pour lives into them generation after generation.

New Orleans' restaurants is too large a subject to cover in 192 pages, or even 300. There are a hundred neighborhood joints with their own family recipes and devoted regulars that deserve to be documented. There are dozens of new places, winning national attention and making history for tomorrow.

For every great restaurant in this book, there are three more I could not include. What I tried to capture is an essence of their histories in the curve of bentwood chairs, the sparkle of stemware, and the black-jacketed elegance of waiters. I photographed rooms full of stories wishing to show a hint of the hidden treasures I hope readers will go find for themselves.

Forgive me for the many things I had to leave out.

New Orleans lost one of its great chefs in 2001, Jamie Shannon of Commander's Palace. In 1999 he was named "#2 Chef in the World" by the *Robb Report* and "Best Chef in the Southeast" by the James Beard Foundation. I am sorry for the even greater history he did not get a chance to make.

I want to thank everyone at the restaurants who helped me and told me their stories. Special thanks to Ted Brennan, Bonnie Warren, and all the generous people at Brennan's; Johnny and Mary Mosca; Colette at Antoine's; and JoAnn at the Upperline.

For various acts of kindness, thank you Emeril, Joe Desalvo, Ellen Johnson, Gil Buras, John Mariani, and Nick Harikiopoulos.

I owe gratitude to Peggy Scott Laborde for her contribution to this project, Mom and Mikko for many editing hours, Debi for the gourmet writing retreat among other things, trainer Noel Authement for helping me not gain fifty pounds, Mara, who was always willing to sample bread pudding, and Joseph Billingsley at Pelican, for coming up with the book idea.

New Orleans' *étouffée* is a mix of onions, celery, sometimes tomatoes, and seasonings cooked down in seafood or chicken stock with shrimp or crawfish. The name comes from the French word for suffocating or sultry and describes the technique of stewing something in a closed saucepan. The rich dish is an obvious metaphor for the city, where, in heat or isolation, a variety of peoples and traditions have been melding deliciously for so many years.

Opposite: *Clancy's "new" wine room*

INTRODUCTION

New Orleans food is as delicious as the less criminal forms of sin.
—Mark Twain

If you were to dream up a city dedicated to carnal pleasures, born to stimulate all five senses, you would surround it with sultry warmth. Maybe place it in a swamp where you can feel the air. Fill it with the dusky perfume of magnolias and jasmine. Give it arched windows and lace-iron balconies. Hide its secrets in brick-paved courtyards with softly splashing fountains and banana trees. Give it jazz.

This city of sensuous bliss would look and act a little like Spain, a little like France, and a little like Havana and Port-au-Prince. It should be on a major port, so the finest from all the world could sidle up to its door.

And fill the tables of this dream to spilling over with rich, spicy, luxurious food and dark sauces, primal food with legs and claws, food that created pearls. Fill the docks with coffee and pineapples from sinfully exotic ports, champagne from France, and rum from Jamaica.

The dream is New Orleans, and its food, like its music and beauty, is a symbol of the inimitable society that created it—European style adapted to a semitropical swamp, influenced by a rainbow of cultures at the dawn of America.

Since Eve ate the apple, much depends on dinner.   —Lord Byron

Thousands of incredible twists and turns of history that led to the unlikely existence of New Orleans made it the ideal atmosphere to foster this dreamland of languid self-indulgence. French explorers, Spanish governors, Choctaw Indians, African slaves, Italian and German immigrants, and the land itself set out the ingredients. The mixture yielded one of the great dining centers of the world, producing America's supreme, if not its only, cuisine.

The savory dream of today started out more like a nightmare. "Eat, drink, and be merry, for tomorrow we die" may truly have been the case for New Orleanians of the eighteenth century. The colony founded in 1718 barely survived in the mosquito-ridden outpost. Hurricanes destroyed most of the town's humble buildings in the early years. And a third of the population died of tropical diseases.

The first New Orleans settlers suffered yellow fever, floods, fires, and isolation, but they would not face the additional hardship of a bland lunch. In 1722 a group of the colony's women, fed up with boring food, marched to Governor Bienville's home, beating pots and kettles with spoons. Bienville said, in effect, "Let them eat filé," and turned them over to his housekeeper and cook, Madame Langlois. She passed on what she had learned from the Indians—the wonders of local spices, vegetables, seafood, and game.

What started as a fiery feminine protest of porridge became known as the Petticoat Rebellion and led, almost three centuries later, to a city that ranks among the top few in the world for dining pleasure, surpassed only by New York and Paris in the *Travel & Leisure* reader's poll of 2001.

The 1938 Federal Writers' Project, *WPA Guide to New Orleans*, says that Spaniards ran the city's first restaurants. The drinks and Spanish dancing at these cafés were, apparently, considerably better than the food.

The WPA guide mentions a few pre-1830s "quieter and more elegant cafés" frequented by Creole gentlemen: Hewlitt's, on Magazine Street in the Banks's Arcade; John Davis's, adjoining his Théâtre d'Orléans; and Maspero's, where the southwest corner of the Omni Royal Orleans Hotel stands today. (A restaurant called Pierre Maspero's currently operates on the opposite corner, 440 Chartres, and claims a founding date of 1788.)

The guide continues, "If a man required good, solid food and was unfortunate enough not to be able to eat at home—the prevailing practice—there was only the *Restaurant d'Orléans* (718 Orleans Street), the exclusive *Le Veau Qui Tête* (919 Decatur), and the somewhat rowdy *Hôtel de la Marine* (next door), haunt of the Lafitte pirates and other colorful characters."

Bethany Ewald Bultman's *Compass Guide to New Orleans* says the city's first recorded restaurant, Café des Emigrés, operated in 1791. John DeMers, in *French Quarter Royalty*, a history of the Omni Royal Orleans Hotel, states that in the early 1800s, Creoles of New Orleans enjoyed a "café society," frequenting the Café des Améliorations, the Café des Emigrés, and the most famous, La Bourse de Maspero, or Maspero's Exchange. DeMers also points out that Maspero's was the most likely candidate of all the saloons claiming to be the meeting place where Andrew Jackson planned the Battle of New Orleans.

At Le Veau Qui Tête, The Suckling Calf, Monsieur Revel offered public baths and reputedly kept the finest stock of wines and liquor in the city. Stanley

Clisby Arthur's 1936 *Old New Orleans: Walking Tours of the French Quarter* says Le Veau Qui Tête operated from 1821 to 1825. In 1833 the building became the new location of the Café des Réfugiés, established in 1808 at 514 St. Philip Street.

While Paul Revere was hanging out at Philadelphia's City Tavern and Parisians dined at La Grande Taverne de Londres, New Orleans cafés were filled with Frenchmen, Spaniards, and newly arrived Creoles from the islands of the Caribbean—exiles, immigrants, and refugees. Food critic Gene Bourg credits the Haitian slave revolt with starting New Orleans' restaurant business, as Creole refugees from the island opened the earliest-known cafés and served Caribbean cuisine.

George Washington Cable, in 1879, wrote of the Café des Exilés shading the banquette of the rue Burgundy at its heyday in 1835. But it was already old then. The owner, M. d'Hemecourt, opened the café when he arrived in New Orleans with thousands of other whites and free men of color fleeing Haiti around 1795. The Café des Exilés competed with the Café des Réfugiés, which Cable places on rue Royal.

When an endless flow of steamboats packed with sugar and cotton made New Orleans rich in the 1830s and 1840s, fine-dining establishments opened to cater to the new wealthy thousands. Two of the grandest hotels in the country, the St. Charles Hotel and the Saint Louis Hotel, employed the best European chefs. Antoine Alciatore, founder of Antoine's Restaurant, worked in the kitchen at the St. Charles Hotel before opening his own pension in 1840. Hotel restaurants were some of the city's best and earliest dining establishments.

Carrollton Gardens, a resort at the end of the New Orleans and Carrollton Railroad line, offered fine dining in the country. On the shore of Lake Pontchartrain, restaurants served French fare on long porches where diners enjoyed the lake breeze.

High-society favorites of this golden age were Moreau's, Victor's (later Galatoire's), and the Gem Coffeehouse at 129 Royal Street, where the first Mardi Gras club, the Mistick Krewe of Comus, was born.

The grand old restaurants that have vanished and those that survive today helped to create the mystique of New Orleans' hidden core, or maybe evolved to accommodate it. Hidden behind a mask of protective walls, drawn damask curtains, and iron gates, New Orleans embraces its reputation for secrecy. New Orleans knows how to seduce, with the just-out-of-reach pleasure—the court-yard glimpsed through a hole in a locked carriageway gate, the always unan-nounced and unrecorded four-A.M. gathering of genius in a back-of-town jazz club, and the ancient French vintages and savory delicacies tasted in the deep-est back chambers of Antoine's or the private dining rooms at Arnaud's.

No one will ever know exactly what political plots and illicit affairs have aris-en between courses at Tujague's and behind the green curtains at Crescent City Steak House.

The oldest restaurants give all five senses a journey back in time. Reflections of white linens in faded mirrors, the tinkling of old silver against old china, and the familiar curve of bentwood chairs beckon the past to coexist with the pres-ent in rooms where Jean Lafitte or Mark Twain might walk through the door.

I once had lunch at Galatoire's with two friends who were dressed as Andrew Jackson and Lola Montez. It scarcely caused a raised eyebrow to sip champagne with a nineteenth-century general and an antebellum dancer on a Friday after-noon at Galatoire's. The air inside is accustomed to swords and petticoats.

Time gets lost here and swept out to sea. Days turn into nights at Antoine's. Lunches turn into dinners at Mr. B's. While in other cities waiters hustle to turn tables twice in one evening, New Orleans restaurants seat groups for lunch that suspends time with levity and they stay through dinner. And then through decades.

Carriage drivers passing by Sbisa and Bayona tell lies about ghost slaves and imagined madams, while the sound of the horseshoes on the old streets tells truths.

Some of the newer restaurants were open when Lindbergh flew across the Atlantic. Their patrons grumbled about Roosevelt's New Deal. Many of the best recent additions to the city's dining scene have roots in much older establish-ments—the chef started at Commander's or the owner is a Brennan. New Orleans is older than the date of it's founding; it is as old as France, as old as Spain, as old as Africa. And in the same way, these restaurants owe their fla-vor to a previous era and long-established tradition.

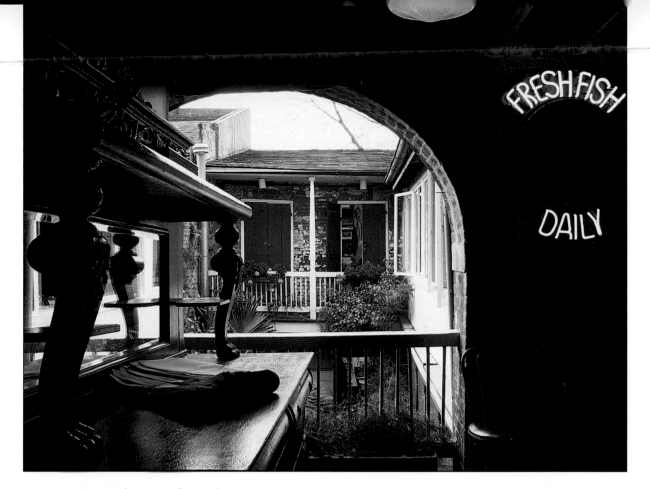

Creole and Cajun

In its original context, the term *Creole* meant a person born in the New World to European parents. However, the word has come to describe anyone of mixed heritage or mixed race. Like the dishes they created, Creole people are a rich blend of the Old and New Worlds.

Creole cuisine, the marriage of French precepts and Louisiana produce, developed throughout the eighteenth and nineteenth centuries in the urban setting of New Orleans. At the same time, in the swamps and along the bayous outside the city, a separate lineage of French descendants was busy at iron pots, inventing Cajun cooking.

A group of exiles descended from rural French fishermen and farmers came to south Louisiana from Acadia, now part of Nova Scotia, beginning in 1755. They had been displaced when British troops forced more than fourteen thousand French Canadians to leave disputed territory at the onset of the Seven Years' War. The refugees who settled west of New Orleans became known as Cajuns, a shortening of the word "Acadians."

While urban Creoles reinvented European haute dishes with refined sauces and imported spices, Cajuns extracted from the bayous and swamps the means to slow-cook hearty, spicy meals. Over time, as a result of interaction with neighboring German immigrants, Cajuns added sausages to their pots.

These are the legacies we enjoy today. From the ultratraditional to the avant-garde, New Orleans restaurants all dip a silver ladle or a wooden spoon into three hundred years of simmering history to incite epicurean ecstasy in the dream city of pleasures.

One cannot think well, love well, sleep well, if one has not dined well.
—Virginia Woolf

NEW ORLEANS' OLDEST RESTAURANTS

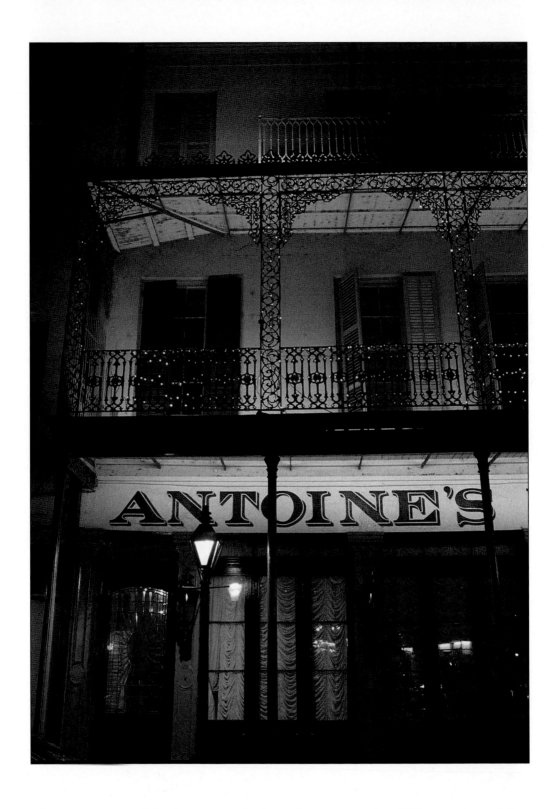

When you want real food go to Antoine's—when you want real life go to New Orleans.
—Herbert Hoover II

Antoine's

At Antoine's you dream in French.

Across a threshold built for horse-drawn carriages, a culinary colossus dressed in lace-iron galleries glows with the yellow light of aged chandeliers.

A waiter in a black dinner jacket carries a dessert shaped like a football to the Dungeon and lights the confection on fire. On the flaming football is the number 1840 in icing.

In a labyrinth of fifteen dining rooms, the walls are filled with ancestral portraits, the glittering accoutrements of New Orleans' nebulous royalty, thousands of celebrity signatures, Groucho Marx's hat, and enough antiquities to fill a museum. A porte-cochère, where time is suspended between day and night, leads from the Mystery Room to the chamber of a sea god.

Presidents, dukes, princesses, and movie stars sit at the dream's tables.

In an infinite corridor of wine, 25,000 bottles lie in fifty-five degrees, while the heat on St. Louis Street melts candles. There's an $800 bottle of nineteenth-century Cognac Otard waiting patiently for the right occasion.

Years ago, the floor in the bright front room was covered with sand. Imported French mirrors came from the Grand Ball Room of the old Saint Louis Hotel. Above this room, Antoine built the bedrooms of his pension, now the Twelfth Night Room.

It has been said that New Orleans without Antoine's would be like Rome without the Coliseum, like Giza without the Great Pyramid.

There is no place like it. Antoine's may be the most famous restaurant in the world. It is the second-oldest restaurant in America, and the oldest still run by its original family. Its founder, Antoine Alciatore, has been credited with practically inventing Creole cooking. Even the current gourmet-coffee craze may have originated when Antoine's began serving its original Café Brulôt Diabolique during Prohibition.

The restaurant's oysters Rockefeller has been called one of the great culinary creations of all time and America's single greatest contribution to haute cuisine.

It seems Antoine's is the living primordial soup where fine dining New Orleans-style began. All good things oozed from the pots of the Pension Alciatore at 50 rue St. Louis.

Napoleon had been dead for only nineteen years, the Civil War was twenty years away, and Texas still belonged to Mexico when Antoine Alciatore opened a boarding house and restaurant on St. Louis Street, not far from the current location, in 1840.

Gas lighting was a relatively new innovation; it would be thirty-nine years before Edison would invent the light bulb. New Orleans' Place d'Armes was yet to be renamed Jackson Square.

Opposite: Antoine's President's Room— where eight U.S. presidents have dined over the years, six while in office.

Antoine Alciatore was born in 1813 in Toulon, France. He began cooking at the age of twelve. As a teenager, Antoine apprenticed at the Hotel de Noailles in Marseilles, where he invented filet Robespierre, grimly named to recall the beheading of the leader of the French Revolution. Antoine's father had witnessed the execution of the man blamed for the Reign of Terror in Paris in 1794 and said Robespierre's face looked like raw beef.

The tasty filet, or maybe the macabre sense of humor, won Antoine a position as chef to the governor of the Chateau d'If, the dreaded island-prison Alexandre Dumas made famous in *The Count of Monte Cristo*.

Antoine came to New Orleans in 1831, and in 1840, the twenty-seven year old opened his pension in a rented building opposite the Saint Louis Hotel, one block from the current location of Antoine's. His upstairs tenants were often performers from the Théâtre d'Orléans on Orleans Street, the center of Creole cultural life.

In 1868 Antoine moved to the 700 block of rue St. Louis to build a larger restaurant, with a boarding house and a residence for his family.

To the New World, Antoine brought *pommes de terre soufflés,* the puffed potatoes invented by mistake by the "Great Chef" Collinet, who was cooking for King Louis Philippe of France. As the story goes, the king arrived late to a celebration dinner and Collinet had to fry his fried potato strips again to reheat them. On the second dunk into the hot oil, to his surprise, they puffed.

In 1874, suffering from tuberculosis, Antoine sailed away from New Orleans to die in his homeland at the age of sixty.

Of Antoine's six sons, Jules would become the new star of his father's restaurant. After learning in the great kitchens of Paris, Strasbourg, and Marseilles, Jules returned to New Orleans in 1887 and took over at Antoine's.

Another son, Fernand, ran a fine Creole restaurant on Iberville Street, La Louisiane, which became one of the city's favorites and a rival of Antoine's.

Jules, during his forty years at Antoine's, invented the restaurant's world-famous dishes, including oysters Rockefeller, the archetypal example of the hybrid that is Creole cuisine—rich French innovation on the half shell.

In the absence of imported escargot, Jules used Louisiana oysters topped with various sauces. In 1899 he made an oyster appetizer, an adaptation of the snails Bourguignonne served by his father, with a covering of vegetable purée—a secret recipe of eighteen ingredients, including absinthe but *not* spinach—so rich that he named it *huîtres en coquilles à la Rockefeller,* after America's wealthiest man.

A side entrance with a telephone provided regulars with a discrete way to call their waiter and avoid the line at the front door.

Opposite: *The Twelfth Night Revelers room, above the main dining room, is the newest addition, remodeled from the old pension accommodations. It honors New Orleans' second-oldest Carnival club, established in 1870.*

Alberto Santos-Dumont, the Brazilian who made aviation history by flying a hydrogen-filled airship around the Eiffel Tower, helped launch a bit of culinary history when Jules created for him pompano *en papillote*, fish cooked in a white paper bag. The bag filled with steam, trapping the flavor and resembling a hot-air balloon.

Legendary Hollywood director Cecil B. DeMille so admired the pompano *en papillote*, he put it in a scene of his 1938 film, *The Buccaneer*, even though the movie about Jean Lafitte and the Battle of New Orleans was set eighty-five years before the pompano first puffed the *papillote* at Antoine's.

In 1908, at a dinner honoring French playwright Victorien Sardou, Jules premiered *œufs Sardou*—poached eggs on steamed artichoke bottoms topped with hollandaise sauce and truffles.

The Knights of Columbus held a dinner at Antoine's in 1921 to celebrate the visit of General Foch, one of the great heroes of World War I. Jules presented a culinary namesake for him, a fried-oysters-and-pâté triumph called *huîtres à la Foch*.

Jules Alciatore's son Roy ran the restaurant for almost forty years until his death in 1972; he was followed by Roy Alciatore, Jr. Antoine's great-grandson, Bernard "Randy" Guste, heads the restaurant today.

Antoine's waiters completely control their tables and have personal business cards. They never write down an order, but keep track of large-party, multicourse meals by memory. For much of the restaurant's history, it took longer to become a waiter at Antoine's than to become a brain surgeon—at one time, the apprenticeship lasted ten years.

Until recently, anyone without a waiter connection could not get a reservation and waited on the banquette on St. Louis Street to dine in the public front room. Relationships with waiters were passed from generation to generation within the Crescent City's upper crust.

Chester, a fifty-year Antoine's veteran, now works alongside two younger generations of his family. Recently, a waiter serving Lisa Marie Presley mentioned to her that he had served her father during the filming of *King Creole* in 1958.

Each of Antoine's dining rooms has its distinct ambience and individual story. The wine room was once the stables. The Mystery Room was a speakeasy. They say, during Prohibition, you could slip into the secret chamber by going through the ladies' room. If someone asked where you got a drink, the answer was, "It's a mystery."

Jules Alciatore, a theatre fan, added the Japanese Room when oriental themes were in fashion and *Madama Butterfly* thrilled the opera audiences of Europe and America. He hired the set builders from the nearby French Opera House to create a setting fit for Cio-Cio-San. The Japanese Room was closed on December 7, 1941, and remained closed for forty-three years. Today it is restored to the last detail of its stained-glass windows and hand-painted bamboo.

In 1942 Roy Alciatore turned an old storeroom into one of the most beautiful of Antoine's spaces. The Rex Room honors the king of Carnival, and the krewe dines there every year on the Wednesday before Mardi Gras.

Real royalty, the duke and duchess of Windsor, feasted in the Rex Room during Mardi Gras in 1949, thirteen years after the duke, as Edward VIII, gave up his throne to marry American divorcée Wallis Warfield Simpson.

Iron bars in the passageway known as the Dungeon survive as evidence of its former life as a colonial prison.

In her glamorous 1948 novel, *Dinner at Antoine's,* Frances Parkinson Keyes uses the private dining rooms of the restaurant as a stage for high-society intrigue. Roy Alciatore appears as himself in the work of fiction. Keyes gives an alternative explanation for the name of the Mystery Room, which involves the disappearance of a lewd work of art.

Fans of the novel sometimes request a recreation of the opening scene in Keyes' mystery. The management obliges with an evening that includes cocktails in the Rex Room and dinner in the 1840 Room. They even use Antoine's legendary duck press.

The paneling in the Roy Alciatore Room (formerly the Capital Room), as well as the mantel and the beams in the ceiling, came from the old state capitol rooms in the Saint Louis Hotel (now the Omni Royal Orleans), when the seat of state government was moved from New Orleans to Baton Rouge in 1882.

Opposite: *The 1840 Room is a replica of one of Antoine's original private dining rooms. Portraits of the Alciatore family hang on the red walls, and the collection of artifacts includes menus from the early 1880s, theatre programs containing Antoine's advertisements as far back as 1852, a Confederate sword, and one of Edison's first light bulbs.*

Another room at Antoine's that honors an old-line Mardi Gras krewe, the Proteus Room, holds treasures of the club established in 1881.

Tujague's

Not long after Antoine Alciatore's pension souffléed its first *pommes de terre,* a Bavarian girl named Elizabeth Kettenring arrived at the New Orleans docks and put her culinary talent on New Orleans' table. From a small second-floor kitchen on *rue de la Levée* (now Decatur Street), Ms. Kettenring won the hearts and stomachs of the city's busy riverfront neighborhood, feeding the masculine midmorning appetites of laborers in the French Market.

According to Stanley Clisby Arthur's 1936 *Old New Orleans: Walking Tours of the French Quarter,* twenty-two-year-old Elizabeth came to New Orleans to join her brother, a French Market butcher, in 1853. She got a job cooking at Louis Dutrey's Coffee House, across the street from the market on the site of the old colonial armory, where she performed culinary wonders with a long-handled skillet. Pretty soon, she married the boss.

Elizabeth's famed "second breakfasts" started a New Orleans tradition still sizzling today in the likes of elaborate breakfasts at Brennan's and brunches at the Court of Two Sisters. Her morning menu included red wine, French bread, onion soup, mayonnaise of celery and shrimps, brisket of beef with horseradish, sweetbread omelets, oyster omelets, stuffed tomatoes, stewed veal tongue with ham, strawberries with Madeira wine, and deliciously on and on.

Dutrey died in 1875, and Elizabeth continued to run the restaurant alone. In 1877 she hired a young French bartender, Hypolite Begue. Three years later, Elizabeth married Hypolite and Dutrey's became Begue's.

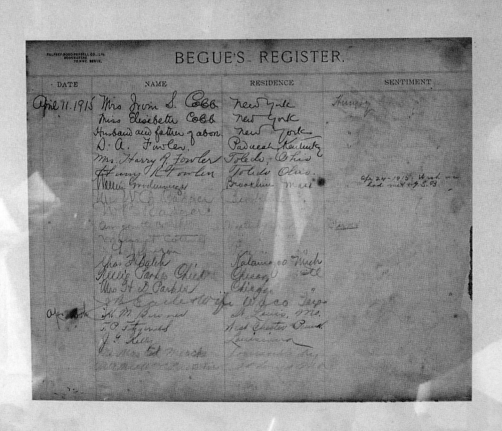

BEGUE'S REGISTER.

The recipes Elizabeth made famous were published in 1900 in a volume titled *Madame Begue's Old New Orleans Cookery.* After Elizabeth Kettenring Dutrey Begue died in 1906, Hypolite remarried, and the second Madame Begue, who had worked in Elizabeth's kitchen, carried on the restaurant.

Today the 1827 building at 823 Decatur combines the histories of two establishments in one space. Guillaume Tujague, a French Market butcher from Mazerolles, France, opened a tavern two doors down from Begue's in 1879. And sometime after World War I, Tujague moved his business into the Begue building.

The current owners of Tujague's, the Latter family, carry on the Begue legacy in the old dining rooms, where multicourse meals take inspiration from the young Bavarian woman's menus.

A garden restaurant at the Royal Sonesta Hotel is named in honor of Madame Begue but has no historical connection to the chef of Tujague's fame.

Tujague's specials board

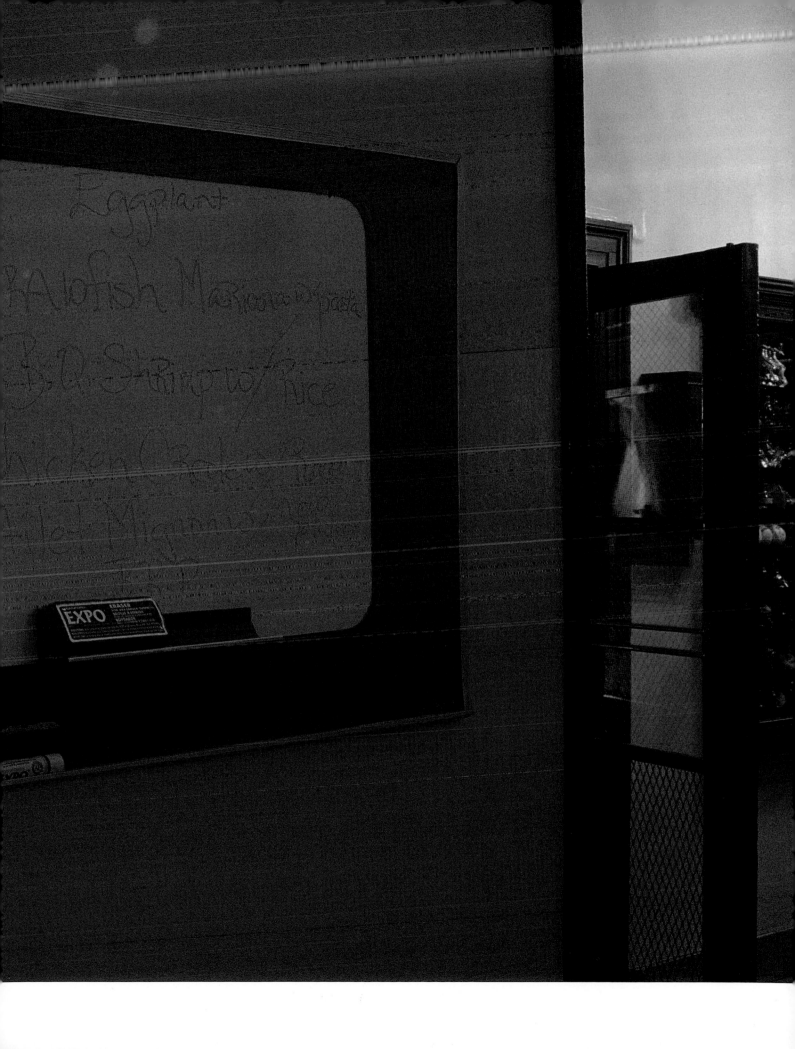

Bruning's

In 1859, Darwin published *The Origin of Species,* John Brown was hanged, and Bruning's began frying fish on New Orleans' lakeshore.

Just a few years after Elizabeth Kettenring arrived from Bavaria and proceeded to cook up Tujague's culinary legacy, another German immigrant, Theodore Bruning, opened a restaurant out on the shore of Lake Pontchartrain, which the fifth and sixth generations of his family run today.

The lakefront attracted New Orleans' leisure class early in the city's history when summer heat closed the theaters and restaurants in town. From the Vieux Carré, a six-mile carriage ride along a shell road ended at New Lake End, now West End, for a cool swim or an outdoor band concert. In 1831 a railroad line connected the city to the lakefront, where a luxurious casino and a beer garden operated. The Pontchartrain Hotel, a fine resort, opened in New Lake End in the 1830s.

The popularity of the lakefront amusements hit its peak in the 1890s, around the time Theodore Bruning's son, known as Cap'n Johnny, inherited the restaurant from his father.

The Cap'n built the Victorian house, still standing behind Bruning's, where, from the widow's walk, he kept a sharp eye on the water. Recently, the Coast Guard gave John C. Bruning its Public Service Award posthumously for his part in rescuing more than two hundred boaters in peril.

Hurricane Georges blew a chunk of the 139-year-old institution off its pilings and into Lake Pontchartrain in 1998. But Bruning's reopened in a two-story building next door that once housed Federico's Bar.

Georges left a few of Bruning's treasures behind—a magnificent 1840 Brunswick bar and a collection of vintage arcade games. Other bits and pieces salvaged from the shallow lake will be back in place when the restaurant is rebuilt.

Inside the temporary building hangs a stuffed hammerhead caught in Florida in 1973 by a longtime Bruning's customer, Brad Glazer.

Beyond the old Bruning's building damaged by the hurricane, pelicans and sea gulls rest on the waves near Cap'n Johnny's 1890s house.

Café Du Monde Coffee Stand

In addition to Antoine's, Tujague's, and Bruning's, one other surviving New Orleans culinary institution predates the Civil War. Actually, a small vending operation called Café Du Monde first served coffee from a French Market stall in 1862, the year Union forces, under the command of Captain Farragut, took the city.

The same riverfront-market community Madame Begue fed with breakfasts of brisket and bordeaux spawned the city's oldest enduring coffee stand. In a part of the French Market previously called Butcher's Hall, Café Du Monde started brewing 140 years ago.

The city's population had grown from 8,000 at the time of the Louisiana Purchase in 1803 to a staggering 170,000 in 1861. New Orleans was the Confederacy's largest and wealthiest town, bustling with businessmen turning cotton into cash. And they all needed a morning coffee or a late-night café au lait.

Unlike the city's 500-plus saloons, referred to as "coffee houses," busily serving absinthe and similar strong spirits in small glasses, stands like Café Du Monde actually filled nineteenth-century New Orleanians with java.

No one knows exactly when Café Du Monde became the large business we know today, or even when beignets were added to the menu, but the famous street café featured French doughnuts by the time Hubert Fernandez bought the business from Fred Koeniger in 1942.

Fernandez, a New Orleans-born Spanish Creole, returned from his job with the United Fruit Company in Honduras after Prohibition and opened Fernandez Wine Cellar in the Pontalba building, across the street from Café Du Monde. Fernandez bought the café and eventually closed his wine shop. His descendants still own the coffee stand today.

New Orleans began receiving shipments of beans from Central and South America early in the 1700s and ranks as America's top coffee importer today. Decades before the name Café Du Monde appeared above a French Market stall, many coffee stands dispensed café noir, café au lait, and pastries around the city, most of them owned by *femmes de couleur.*

Gumbo Ya Ya, a collection of Louisiana folk tales published in 1945, tells of Old Rose, who bought her freedom from slavery and ran a famous coffee stall in the old French Market early in the 1800s. The book says her coffee "was like the benediction that follows after prayer."

According to the folk tales, in the 1840s, children on shopping errands would always save a picayune to buy a tiny cup of sweet coffee from Manette, a quadroon woman who ran a French Market stand.

Chef John Folse says the beignet came to New Orleans in 1727 with the Ursuline nuns and probably derived from the classic French beignets *Viennois.*

The history of the Market itself predates the settlement of the colony. Indians used this high point on the banks of the Mississippi as a trading post well before Bienville decided on a suitable spot for the city.

LATE NINETEENTH CENTURY

After the Civil War, Federal occupation lingered in the city for fifteen years. The booming economy disintegrated, the South lost its slave-based fortune, and carpetbaggers sat in the government offices. But New Orleans would not give up its coffee.

Morning Call Coffee Stand

In 1870 Joseph Jurisich, an immigrant from the region of Yugoslavia that is now Croatia, opened Morning Call Coffee Stand two blocks downriver from Café Du Monde in the old vegetable market and offered some competition in the café-au-lait business.

In the 1930s, Morning Call became a drive-in, serving coffee to customers surrounding the block in new Model Ts and Pierce-Arrows. They had to close for a short time during World War II, when rationing left the doughnuts without the requisite piles of powdered sugar.

A century after Morning Call opened, Mayor Moon Landrieu's beautification of the riverfront area restricted parking around the French Market, so Morning Call moved to Fat City in Metairie, a shopping district that inherited the name, a vernacular synonym for "success," from the Fat City snowball stand that once stood at the corner of Severn and 17th Streets. With the original counters, stools, and arch, the Jurisich family still serves coffee and square doughnuts in nineteenth-century style, magically anachronistic in a 1970s strip mall.

Commander's Palace

#1 restaurant in America —Food & Wine, 1995, 1997, and 2000

Paul Prudhomme, Emeril Lagasse, and Jamie Shannon in succession wore the toque as head chef at Commander's Palace—a powerful legacy indeed. Combine these three superstars of chefdom with the first family of New Orleans restaurants, the Brennans, and you have a turreted, turquoise culinary institution of monumental significance.

This temple of fine dining stands among the palmettos, magnolias, and crumbling grandeur of New Orleans' Garden District. The neighborhood was carved out of the swamp upriver from the French Quarter in the 1700s. Originally a part of the Livaudais sugar plantation, the area became residential as the city's population grew in the 1830s.

The second-floor Garden Room of Commander's Palace looks out across Washington Avenue over a sea of whitewashed tombs. Lafayette Cemetery, established in 1833, covers two blocks and contains a chronicle of the notorious nineteenth-century yellow-fever epidemics in which thousands died while terrified citizens burned tar and fired cannons to chase the disease from the city.

In 1880, when Emile Commander opened his restaurant to serve haute Creole dishes to Uptown's elite, New Orleans was again enjoying wealth after Reconstruction. Storyville had recently been established in an attempt to limit the sex trade geographically, and a melting pot of musical traditions simmered in New Orleans clubs and cathouses on the way to becoming jazz.

Elsewhere in America, Custer and 264 of his men had been slaughtered at Little Big Horn in 1876, Mark Twain was about to introduce the world to Huck Finn in 1884, and a gift from France—*Liberty Enlightening the World,* later called the Statue of Liberty—would soon be shipped to New York in 1886.

Around 1915, Commander sold his restaurant to the Giarrantano family, who ran the restaurant with some added amenities in the 1920s. According to *Great Restaurants of the World, Commander's Palace,* riverboat captains and sporting gentlemen met with beautiful women for rendezvous in the private dining rooms upstairs, using a back entrance, while respectable families gathered for after-church lunches downstairs. Commander's racy reputation continued into the thirties when its private dining booths shrouded clandestine liaisons.

Opposite: *The second floor of Commander's Palace—Marilyn Carter Rougelot painted the floral yellow walls of the Coliseum Room.*

Top: *Commander's kitchen*

Opposite: *Frank and Elinor Moran owned the restaurant from 1944 until the Brennan's took over in 1969. Elinor Moran created the garden patio, where she kept a talking mynah bird named Tajar. The bird became so famous that he even appeared on* Candid Camera.

Emeril's Delmonico

Emile Commander's Palace had impressed Garden District gourmets for more than a decade when another Commander dipped his ladle into the Uptown dining pot. In 1895, Anthony Commander opened Delmonico's on St. Charles Avenue. He named it after the oldest restaurant in America, New York's Delmonico's, which first served elegant lunches to Manhattan businessmen in the 1820s.

During the 1890s, the St. Charles streetcar switched from mule power to electricity and the avenue filled up with magnificent mansions. New Orleans' legendary architects like Emile Weil, Thomas Sully, and partners Favrot and Livaudais designed homes for cotton kings and river barons who desired addresses on the newly fashionable thoroughfare.

Ownership of New Orleans' Delmonico's passed to Anthony LaFranca in 1911 and stayed in the LaFranca family for eighty-five years. The 1890 building, originally a one-story dairy creamery, gained a second floor sometime before LaFranca took over.

While the restaurant operated downstairs, LaFranca turned the second floor into a boxing gym, reflecting New Orleans' growing passion for the sport. Louisiana was the first state in the Union to legalize prize fighting in 1891. Many famous bouts were fought in the city, and in 1917, a New Orleans native, Pete Herman, won the world championship. Today sepia photographs of the early twentieth century hang in the piano bar showing old Delmonico's patrons and boxers in the second-floor gym.

Emeril Lagasse purchased Delmonico's from Anthony LaFranca's daughters, Angie and Rose, a century after its founding. The restaurant is now Emeril's Delmonico, a sophisticated, updated version of the classic Creole landmark. New Orleans' top design firm, Holden and Dupuy, created the new look at Delmonico's. The second-story Anthony Room and Rose Room bear the names of their former residents.

Café Sbisa

Back in the French Market area that gave birth to Tujague's and Café Du Monde, Café Sbisa numbers among New Orleans' few enduring nineteenth-century treasures. Sbisa opened its doors in 1899 and today pours a hundred years of tradition into its court-bouillon and hot Creole bread pudding.

The restaurant remained in the Sbisa family almost eighty years, and except for a three-year period in the 1990s, the café has been in continuous operation. The time-worn building housed a second-floor residence in the 1820s above a ship's outfitter on the first.

Inside Sbisa's dining room of aged wood and crumbling brick lurks a spirit of Bacchanalian flirtation, given life in George Dureau's giant painting. The depiction of Sbisa's grand bar hangs above the scene it portrays.

Sbisa's second-floor loggia

Acme Oyster House

Man's passion for the mollusk began before recorded time. Ancient civilizations left enormous mounds of shells as monuments to their beloved little globs of protein.

Millennia before European explorers set foot on the continent, Native Americans enjoyed the unassuming bi-valve that would one day give Casanova his *je ne sais quoi.*

Around the turn of the twentieth century in America, advances in cold-storage technology widened the availability of raw oysters, already one of New Orleans' favorite dishes. Soon the city would be on the road to that distinctive ecstasy of horseradish mixed with ketchup, Worcestershire, Tabasco, and lemon juice in a little paper cup with Lance saltines in plastic wrappers, Dixie beer, and a tray of cold, raw "ersters."

Acme Oyster and Seafood House, originally called the Acme Café, started shucking in 1910 at 117 Royal Street, next to the old Cosmopolitan Hotel. A century ago, this block was a hot spot of social and political life. Arthur's *Old New Orleans* says, "Many a Central American revolution was hatched by Spanish-speaking guests" at the Cosmopolitan's St. Regis restaurant. A few doors down stood the famous Gem Saloon, birthplace of the Mistick Krewe of Comus. Across the street, at the original Sazerac Coffeehouse, eighteen bartenders served New Orleans' whiskey cocktail sensation at a 125-foot bar.

When Acme opened, its patrons might have been curious to try the relatively new Dixie Beer. New Orleans' oldest brewery was just three years old in 1910 and had thirteen other local brands to compete with.

In 1924, 117 Royal Street burned down, and Acme moved around the corner to 724 Iberville, an 1814 building where the ninety-year-old oyster house keeps on shuckin'.

Arnaud's

The year 1918 brought the end of World War I, the close of Storyville, and the dawn of Prohibition. New Orleans celebrated its 200th anniversary and, more importantly, the opening of Arnaud's.

Speaking of stressful "modern life" at the time, Count Arnaud reminded diners that "eating should be a pleasure, not a task to get over with in a hurry. A dinner chosen according to one's needs, tastes, and moods, well prepared and well served, is a joy to all senses and an impelling incentive to sound sleep, good health, and long life."

Since then, thousands have experienced the joy of shrimp Arnaud and oysters Bienville. And if Arnaud's fine food and atmosphere doesn't make life longer, it certainly makes life better.

Leon Bertrand Arnaud Cazenave, a child of Bosdaros, France, came to America via Paris, planning to become a doctor. He enrolled in Saint Stanislaus College in Bay Saint Louis, Mississippi. But medical school was not in destiny's cupboard for this flamboyant Frenchman. According to family lore, Cazenave could not afford the expense of medical school, and his English was below par. So, with his sparkling personality and knowledge of French vineyards, he instead put his efforts into the wine business.

Opposite: *Portraits of the Count; his wife, Lady Irma; and daughter, Germaine, watch over Arnaud's main dining room, one of the grandest spaces in the French Quarter. Original chandeliers, fans, iron columns, and Italian tile floors remain in place. The new owner, Archie Casbarian, had the old tin ceiling replicated. Silver, glassware, and china patterns are those chosen by the Count himself. Buzzers, used to summon waiters in the small second floor private rooms, still work.*

Cazenave came to New Orleans as a champagne salesman in 1902, found the French style of the city suited him, and decided to stay. He pursued his wish to own his own restaurant. Cazenave's first café was at 240 Bourbon Street, where he leased the Old Absinthe House and served French meals with a free *demi-bouteille* of wine.

In 1918 Cazenave bought an old warehouse on Bienville Street and built his famous namesake. He ruled over the lavish Creole establishment like a magnanimous royal, drank champagne every day for breakfast, and stayed out all night on Bourbon Street with friends. Somewhere along the line, his grand and elegant style earned him the nickname "Count."

During Prohibition, federal authorities barely kept from drowning in the sea of liquor in New Orleans, where the law was all but ignored. The Count, like all gourmets, considered wine an integral part of fine dining and had a personal passion for spirits. He reportedly drank twenty cups of bourbon and coffee (half and half) per day, after the champagne, of course.

Cazenave refused to abide by the new law and paid several fines in the 1920s. But when undercover agents acquired drinks at the restaurant, the extravagant Count and two of his waiters went to jail. The restaurant was padlocked. Agents even raided Cazenave's mansion on Esplanade Avenue, taking all of his rare bottles.

Cazenave was indicted on twenty-seven charges, but a jury failed to convict him. Soon, the Volstead Act would be repealed.

When Cazenave bought the warehouse that would become Arnaud's, houses of prostitution and drug dens populated the area. But the unsavory neighbors did not hamper the success of the restaurant, and slowly, Cazenave purchased the surrounding properties. The main building dates to 1883 and connects to eleven other nineteenth-century structures. They say that ghosts of opium fiends chill the air in the Richelieu Bar, one of the oldest of the conjoined buildings.

DO NOT ENTER
THE DINING ROOM
AREAS UNLESS YOU
ARE IN UNIFORM!!

NO EXCEPTIONS

In Arnaud's surreal museum, mannequins display
Germaine's French-made ball dresses.
Top, left: Germaine wore a gown representing
vintage champagne as Queen of Sparta in 1954.
The whole court dressed as delicious dishes and
fine wine.
Top, right: Another of Germaine's ethereal gowns,
this one entitled "Paris."

Opposite: "Woman of the World" (Germaine's
gown as Queen of Nayades, 1960)—For
Germaine Cazenave Wells, the party never
ended. She even went to the grave in her
favorite gold lamé Mardi Gras gown.

Count Arnaud's seditious spunk and self-propelled fame extended to his daughter, Germaine Cazenave Wells, a slightly scandalous, completely brazen local celebrity and queen of twenty-two Mardi Gras balls.

In a *New Orleans Times-Picayune* interview, Germaine's costumer, Larry Youngblood, told of an incident at a Mardi Gras ball in the fifties between the queen and her king, state senator Dudley LeBlanc: "The instant they met for the grand march, Miss Wells took a vicious dislike to Mr. LeBlanc and swatted him in the crotch with her sceptre. . . . They both had mouths on them that would make a truck driver blush."

After her father's death in 1948, Germaine, Cazenave's only child, became the owner of Arnaud's. During Germaine's tenure, Arnaud's was named one of the top five restaurants in the world by a Paris newspaper, and Arnaud's Jean Pierre was included in an elite group of the world's five best chefs, chosen to participate in a New York celebration of the 2,000th birthday of Paris.

In 1978 Germaine chose her successor at Arnaud's, Archie Casbarian, not because he was one of the world's top hoteliers, but because he reminded her of her father. The well-dressed, French-speaking connoisseur even has the same initials as Cazenave.

Broussard's

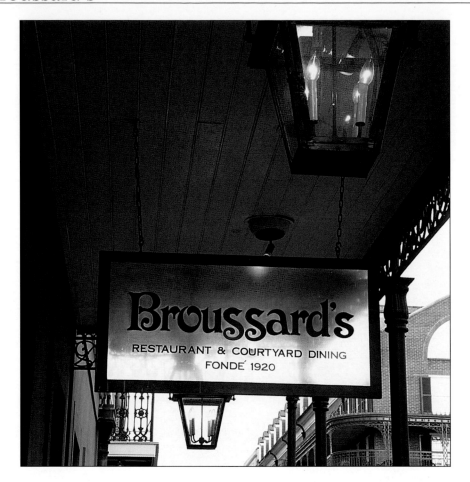

Papa Joe Broussard had a bad temper and a Napoleon obsession. At his French Quarter restaurant, Broussard reputedly threw plates of unsatisfactory food out the kitchen door and onto Conti Street. When a customer ordered Napoleon brandy, a bell was rung, the lights dimmed, and the waiters gathered around a statue of the emperor to sing the *Marseillaise.* Thus, Joseph Broussard entertained and fed New Orleans while honoring Napoleon for forty-six years.

Joseph, a French Creole, started his culinary career at Antoine's in the early 1900s, where he learned from Jules Alciatore, the son of Antoine's founder and the most famous chef in the South.

Broussard's marriage to Rosalie Borrello brought him to the 1834 Borrello mansion in the 800 block of Conti. The couple moved in upstairs and opened the restaurant downstairs in 1920. Since then, Broussard's has expanded to incorporate an impressive collection of historic buildings.

Broussard's large property backs up to the 1831 Hermann-Grima house, now a museum home on the National Register of Historic Places. Broussard's Josephine and Magnolia dining rooms occupy the old washroom, stables, and slave quarters of the Hermann-Grima mansion. Part of Broussard's property was the site of the Jefferson Academy, an exclusive boys school that operated here from 1835 to 1885.

Today Broussard's is owned and operated by Gunter and Evelyn Preuss. One of New Orleans' great chefs, Gunter Preuss was born in Berlin and came to New Orleans with his family to head the Sazerac Restaurant at the Fairmont Hotel in 1967.

Opposite and above: *Broussard's main dining room looks out on Papa Joe's Napoleon Patio, now simply Broussard's courtyard, often called the most beautiful in the French Quarter. It contains the Quarter's oldest and largest wisteria.*

Left: *Broussard's Josephine Room, the old slave quarters of the Hermann-Grima house.*

Broussard's courtyard

The Charm Gate in the carriageway of the Court of Two Sisters.
According to legend, Queen Isabella had these gates blessed so
their charm would pass to anyone who touched them.

The Court of Two Sisters

The celebrated sisters, Emma Camors Musso and Bertha Camors Angaud, opened a notions shop at 613 Royal Street in 1886. In their Shop of the Two Sisters, they sold buttons, thread, French lace, ribbons, fans, frills, and other tiny niceties in a grand mansion with an even grander garden.

The home had been built in 1818 for Jean Baptiste Zenon Cavelier, president of the Banque d'Orleans, by the preeminent architect-builders of the time, Claude Gurlie and Joseph Guillot.

The proper ladies somehow became subjects of some bizarre rumors. People said they cavorted with Jean Lafitte, who killed three pirates beneath the courtyard trees, and that a tunnel connected the courtyard to other pirate hideouts. Unfortunately, Jean's French Quarter buccaneering days ended decades before the Camors sisters were born, and below-ground travel seems unlikely in the swampy soil of New Orleans, but dramatic settings elicit elaborate myths.

The shop closed in 1906, and twenty-eight years later Nola Mize and Mrs. Zula Sturgis opened a restaurant named for the Camors sisters in the Cavelier mansion.

In the 1980s, almost a century after the Camors provided finishing touches to the blouses of French Quarter ladies, two brothers decided to find out what became of the two sisters. Present-day owners of the Court of Two Sisters restaurant, Joe and Jerry Fein, compelled by their connection to the women whose legend gave the Court its name, discovered that the sisters had died in poverty a few months apart in 1944. The final resting place of Emma and Bertha was a dilapidated, unidentified tomb in Saint Louis Cemetery No. 3. The Fein brothers paid thousands of dollars to refurbish the tomb, which had been scheduled for destruction, and they frequently visit the cemetery with flowers for the sisters.

MANGIA ITALIANO

At the end of the nineteenth century, New Orleans got a big plate of Italian culture. By 1890, 15,000 Italians lived in the city, the majority from the poverty-stricken island of Sicily. The French Quarter became an Italian quarter, as Creoles moved out and the new immigrants moved in.

Brocato's

In 1905 an Italian immigrant named Gennaro Lombardi introduced pizza to New York City. Coca-Cola changed its recipe, replacing cocaine with caffeine. Einstein posited that time and space are relative to the observer. And Picasso experimented with cubism.

About the same time in New Orleans, a young Italian named Angelo Brocato brought a sweet little slice of Palermo to the French Quarter, founding the oldest ice-cream parlor in Louisiana.

Joseph Brocato had already established himself as an ice-cream vendor in the city when his brother, Angelo, arrived from Palermo to join him. The Brocato boys, like many Sicilian men, did hard labor in Louisiana sugarcane fields during harvests to earn money to bring family members to the New World.

In 1902, Joseph and Angelo opened an ice-cream parlor together in the 1200 block of Decatur Street, using recipes and traditions they learned growing up in Sicily. This was not easy work either. Making ice cream by hand required a strong arm.

In 1905 Angelo opened his own shop in the 500 block of Ursuline Street and decorated it in the finest Palermo style. His was one of the first New Orleans ice-cream parlors with café tables and chairs so customers could sit and socialize while sharing a cold torroncino or lemon ice. In 1921 the shop moved to the 600 block of Ursuline, where it stayed for sixty years.

Ursuline Street between Royal and Chartres streets eventually became known as "Spumone Block" for its Italian ice-cream and sweet shops. Today the old Brocato's is the home of Croissant d'Or, a French patisserie, but the look of the old Italian ice-cream parlor remains.

Angelo Brocato's Carrollton location opened in 1980. The tile floor and tables came with the family from the French Quarter and date to 1921. They still serve spumone in slices, the way Italian ice cream was served before the cone. From ancient recipes, seed cookies, buccellati, and dead man's bones fill antique jars and glass cases.

The grandson of Angelo, Arthur Brocato, carries on the family tradition today with the help of his older brother, Angelo, Jr., and uncle, Roy, Angelo, Sr.'s youngest son. Several other Brocatos are involved in the business, including members from the fourth generation.

Central Grocery

Just one year after young Angelo Brocato introduced New Orleans to the frozen delights of Palermo, Lupo Salvadore, from Cefalù, Sicily, offered a cornucopia of Italian pastas, olive oil, spices, meats, and cheeses to the large Italian community surrounding the French Market.

Generations of New Orleanians have developed an almost perverse passion for the sandwich that Salvadore made at his grocery counter: the muffuletta—a large, round Italian loaf stuffed with layers of ham, salami, and cheeses, and piled with olive salad. Muffuletta is a Sicilian surname, so chances are Lupo named the sandwich for a friend or customer.

Salvadore's grandson, Tommy Tusa, and Tommy's cousins Frank and Larry Tusa, continue the tradition of savory Italian imports and still make muffulettas that keep locals lining up down the sidewalk on Decatur Street every day at lunchtime.

Napoleon House

Five blocks over from Central Grocery, on the corner of Chartres and St. Louis streets, another Italian grocery operated in the old Girod mansion, known as the Napoleon House because of its link to a famous local plot to rescue Bonaparte from exile. In 1914, the Impastato family bought the corner grocery that eventually became one of the greatest bars in America.

Though today the Napoleon House is better known for its opera music and Pimm's cups, the menu at Girod's Bistro, the Napoleon House restaurant, is worthy of its French-imperial stature. And the Impastatos make one of the best muffulettas in town.

Fiorella's

Another survivor of the French Quarter's Italian era, Fiorella's Café, opened in 1937. The turn-of-the-century building started out as a riverfront gambling house where lonely sailors could take their chances with craps and cards downstairs and, with any luck, spend their winnings on the ladies upstairs.

Rocco "Rocky" Tommaseo, the grandson of Rocky Tommaseo, one of the founders of Rocky and Carlo's restaurant in Chalmette, recently bought Fiorella's.

Pascal's Manale

The New Orleans and Carrollton Railroad started running in 1835 and slowly brought residential development to the plantation land upriver from the city that would become Uptown.

The steam train, running to the town of Carrollton along the current route of the St. Charles Avenue streetcar, made a halfway stop on the Bouligny plantation. Developers subdivided the land into lots in the 1830s and named the new neighborhood's grandest avenue after the grandest Frenchman, hero to New Orleans French Creoles—Napoleon.

By the second decade of the twentieth century, mansions lined St. Charles Avenue. Tulane had moved in across from Audubon Park in 1894, and Loyola University opened next door in 1912. Also during that year, the world was shocked by the sinking of the unsinkable *Titanic*. Speaking of ice, home refrigerators went on the market about the same time. The iceman would soon be out of work.

In 1913 Frank Manale founded his Sicilian Creole restaurant on the old Bouligny tract. His nephew, Pascal Radosta, took over when Manale died in 1937. Today the combination of their names glows in neon under the oak trees on Napoleon Avenue.

Radosta got together with his brother Jake and a friend, Vincent Sutro, on a Sunday afternoon in 1954 and created one of the city's foremost original dishes—barbecued shrimp. He called it "barbecued" because of its spicy, rich sauce, but the dish actually wasn't barbecued at all. The unpeeled shrimp were baked in a peppered mixture of beer and butter, so messy that it came with a red-embroidered cloth bib. Paper bibs have replaced the cloth ones, but the tangy specialty still entices shrimp lovers today.

After ninety years, Pascal's Manale remains in the family. Radosta's daughter Virginia owns the business with her husband, Savare De Felice, and their four children. The next generation, Pascal Radosta's great-grandchildren and the future owners of the famous Uptown restaurant, are now starting at the bottom of the ladder like all family members before them. Thomas washes pots, David is an apprentice chef, and Trey waits tables.

Casamento's

Three of New Orleans best-loved oyster emporia, Acme, Pascal's Manale, and Casamento's, all began shucking in the same decade.

In 1919 Joe Casamento built the famous Magazine Street mollusk heaven, where they still use cast-iron pots to fry seafood in lard. The bright light of vintage art-deco fluorescent fixtures lends a celestial aura to oyster sandwiches, oyster stew, and just plain oysters.

Joe Casamento's children, Mary Ann and Joseph, followed in their father's footsteps. Joseph, in his seventies, is about ready to retire but still operates the cash register and helps shuck oysters. He still puts up ladders in the dining room and climbs onto planks between them to brush down the walls the way Casamentos have done since 1949. The floor tile is the 1919 original. In the summer of 1949, the family closed the restaurant to install the wall tile, and the tradition of summer holiday began. They enjoyed the break and have closed for the summer ever since, not because the oysters aren't good in the summer, but rather to relax.

C. J. Gerdes, Mary Ann's son, takes the family business into the third generation. He runs the restaurant with his wife, Linda, who has been a Casamento's waitress for twenty years.

Domilise's

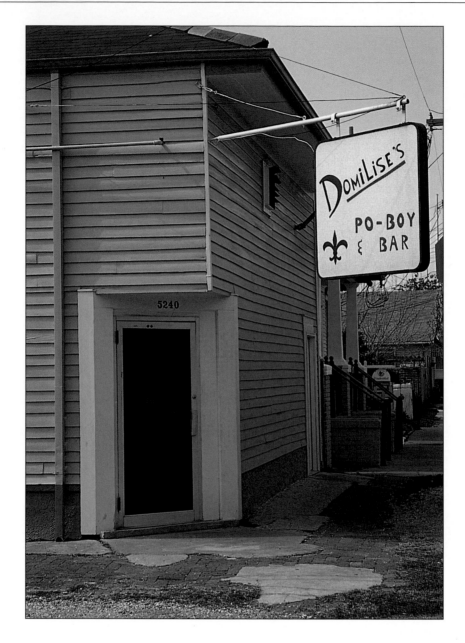

In 1927 Peter Domilise opened a bar near the river Uptown, across the street from his mother's grocery store. Peter's son Sam took over his father's neighborhood joint in the fifties.

Sam's wife, Dot, is the acknowledged po' boy genius of the Domilise clan. Dot runs the famous lunch spot with her daughter-in-law Pat, loading countless loaves with homemade roast beef and lightly fried seafood.

Diners from all over town line up at the old corner saloon for Dot's oyster-and-shrimp po'boys, hot-sausage po'boys, and gravy-soaked roast-beef po' boys

One of the critical features of the perfect New Orleans neighborhood po' boy, at Domilise's and almost everywhere else, is Leidenheimer's French bread. G. H. Leidenheimer came from Germany in 1896 and started baking golden loaves, with just the right softness on the inside and crunch on the outside, in New Orleans' Central City.

Mandina's

For thirty years, waiter Kenneth Julian has been sloshing generous doses of sherry into the steaming bowls of Mandina's famous turtle soup. Dishes stack up on the bus trays with barely a drop of rum sauce left from the bread pudding. Regulars linger after lunch, sipping manhattans, one boot propped on the old brass foot rail. And everyone in the place stops to cheer when the Saints score a touchdown on television.

In 1898 Sebastian Mandina, from Salaporati, Sicily, opened a corner grocery at Canal and Cortez streets, in a growing working-class neighborhood around the Mid-City factories. He and his family lived above the typical turn-of-the-century storehouse where the streetcars passed on the way to the "Cemeteries" terminus.

Mandina's corner store was a popular combination grocery and pool hall in the early decades of the twentieth century. When Sebastian died in 1932, his sons Frank and Anthony turned the space into a restaurant.

During World War II, Frank and Anthony fought in Europe, and Anthony's wife, Miss Hilda, ran the restaurant alone. When the Mandina boys returned in 1946, Anthony resumed his place in the kitchen and Frank behind the bar.

Frank sold his half of the business to the family to pay his debts in the 1960s after a run of bad luck at the racetrack. He still hung around the restaurant and lived upstairs in an apartment next door to his brother. The streetcars stopped running on Canal Street in 1964, around the time the next Mandina restaurateur was born.

Anthony's son Tommy is the fourth generation, supervising the family business with help from a fifth-generation member, his daughter Cindy. Cindy plans to lead Mandina's into a new century by keeping the neighborhood's beloved repository of old-New Orleans nostalgia exactly the same. Red beans and rice with Italian sausage is the Monday special, just as it was fifty years ago, and the spaghetti and meatballs and trout almandine stay the same generation after generation.

Charlie's Steak House

Charlie Petrossi, an immigrant from Ustica, Sicily, founded Charlie's Steak House in 1932. The prime rib, au-gratin potatoes, and the city's best blue-cheese dressing have kept diners coming to this windowless Uptown road-house for seventy years.

Petrossi's daughter, Dottye Petrossi Bennett, started waiting tables at her dad's restaurant in 1952 and still serves up T-bones and big fries in her seventies. Dot's brother, Charlie, Jr., has run the business since Charlie, Sr., died in 1976.

Liuzza's Lounge and Grill

The Union Race Course, laid out in 1852 in the swampy outskirts of New Orleans, is the oldest racetrack still galloping in America. Today, the 145-acre venue, known as the Fair Grounds, is home to a winter season of eighty-eight race days. But entertainment at the track is not limited to horses: among other events, the Fair Grounds hosts the world-famous New Orleans Jazz and Heritage Festival.

In the past, audiences at the arena also saw more than just thoroughbred racing. During the Civil War, promoters of various sports leased the track. In 1863 the events included boxing, baseball, and bull-and-bear fights.

Jack Liuzza opened a combination bar, grocery, and bookie joint in an old Victorian house near the racetrack in 1936. The saloon, frequented by jockeys and race fans, stayed in the Liuzza family for half a century, as Jack's son and grandson took the reins.

Jack's grandson, also named Jack, stopped selling groceries around 1965, when supermarkets came on the scene. He renamed the place Liuzza's Lounge and Grill.

In 1996 Billy Gruber and Jimmy Lemarie leased the bar from the Liuzza family and gave it a culinary giddyap. Gruber has the business in his bloodline. His father, state senator Bill Gruber, started a New Orleans institution called Meal-A-Minit in 1935, one of the city's first fast-food chains. But Gruber says the zip in his gumbo comes from his mother's Cajun pedigree. Her maiden name is Boudreaux.

Liuzza's by the track has no known family tie to another favorite neighborhood restaurant called Liuzza's that opened on Bienville Street in the 1940s.

THE CROATIAN KITCHEN

In the early decades of the twentieth century, during political upheaval in southeastern Europe, many immigrants from the Balkan coast settled in Louisiana, where they worked as fishermen, effectively creating New Orleans' oyster industry. Not long after, several Croatian-owned oyster and seafood places opened, including Uglesich's, Bozo's, Andrew Jaeger's, Drago's, and Gentilich's (now Peristyle).

Other local culinary landmarks owe their existence to the downfall of Austria-Hungary as well, including Morning Call Coffee Stand, the original Chris Steak House, and Crescent City Steak House.

Mandich

The corner bar established by a Croatian immigrant named John Mandich in 1922 had humble culinary beginnings—sandwiches and raw oysters. But today, the pink "Galatoire's of the Ninth Ward" stirs up raves from *Gourmet* magazine and *Saveur*.

In 1947 Mandich's nephew, Anthony Matulich, and a partner, Lloyd "Bubby" English, bought the place. English's wife, Nimber Arthur English, took over the kitchen, where she did wonderful things to seafood for twenty-five years.

The neighborhood surrounding Mandich has changed drastically, but inside the restaurant, the last forty years seem to disappear. The dining room was expanded in the 1960s, but since then, the menu and the décor have stayed the same.

Lloyd English, Jr., runs the place as his father did before him. His wife, Joel, took over the kitchen in 1972. She continues to draw diners into Bywater with her mother-in-law's famous recipes for trout Mandich, oysters Bordelaise, and sweet-potato duck.

Uglesich's

A dilapidated shack on a lost corner in Central City, across the street from the century-old Brown's Velvet Dairy, has risen to star status in the local lunch scene. Every afternoon a discriminating crowd, often with celebrities and great New Orleans chefs among them, packs into the ten tables between stacks of boxes and the oyster bar to satisfy a craving for one-of-a-kind po' boys and fried green tomatoes with shrimp rémoulade.

Sam Uglesich, from the island of Dugi Otok in Croatia, opened his first sandwich shop on South Rampart Street in 1924, not long after Benny and Clovis Martin invented the famous five-cent "poor boy" sandwich to feed striking streetcar workers. Uglesich moved to the current location in 1927.

Anthony Uglesich, the founder's son, runs the restaurant today. A handwritten menu hangs on the wall, listing the classic daily specials, sandwiches, and seafood, but Anthony and his wife, Gail, have also created new dishes and raised Uglesich's fare to neighborhood-joint gourmet, or haute shack. Uglesich's oyster po' boy, with fat, shucked, and fried-to-order oysters, is enough to bring fans back week after week and year after year.

Bottom: *Michael Rogers stands shucking behind Uglesich's tiny oyster bar. One of the award plaques behind him says 1st Prize, Best Shucker in New Orleans, 2001 Louisiana Oyster Convention.*

Ruth's Chris Steak House

Ruth Fertel was browsing the newspaper for entrepreneur opportunities in 1965, when an ad reading "Steakhouse for sale" caught her eye. Against the advice of her banker, the divorced mother of two, with no knowledge of the restaurant business, decided to mortgage her home and buy Chris Steak House.

The little Broad Street restaurant that would become a multi-million-dollar international business had Croatian origins. An immigrant named Chris Matulich founded Chris Steak House in 1927. At the time, Broad Street (Highway 90) was on the main thoroughfare linking the states along the Gulf Coast from Florida to Texas.

Fertel left her job as a lab assistant at Tulane University School of Medicine, where she earned $4,800 a year, to try her hand at the restaurant business. Matulich and Fertel agreed that the name would remain only as long as it occupied the original location.

Under the direction of the young Fertel, Chris Steak House gained momentum. After a fire destroyed the original building in 1976, Fertel moved four blocks and named the new restaurant Ruth's Chris Steak House. The masculine, unpretentious home of hot-buttered steak became the regular lunch spot of politicians, Saints players, and every meat lover in town.

As her success sizzled, Fertel opened Ruth's Chris restaurants in other cities and eventually sold franchises. When Fertel sold the business in 1999, she left more than eighty locations generating over $330 million annually.

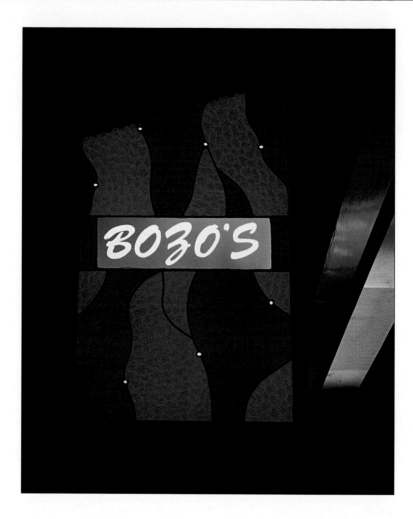

Bozo's is yet another Croatian culinary gift to the city. Bozo (an Americanization of the Croatian name *Boja*) and Marie Vodanovich founded the restaurant on St. Ann and North Broad streets in 1928, the same year that Huey P. Long was elected governor.

Bozo loved horses and owned a couple of thoroughbreds. Many jockey friends and trainers from the Fair Grounds racetrack hung out at the restaurant. Doug Atkins, Dave Rowe, and other Saints greats downed martinis and raw oysters with Bozo's patrons. Pete Fountain's dad worked behind the bar.

Bozo's son Chris, also called Bozo, took the family's secret recipes and reputation for perfectly prepared seafood out to the suburbs in 1979, abandoning the old location for a large, modern Metairie building, placing old New Orleans flavor in disco-era suburbia. The football stars still visit when they're in town, and Pete Fountain's children are regular customers. Photographs of racehorses fill the walls of the bar.

You can't swing a catfish without hitting a Vodanovich in this family-owned establishment. Bozo's wife, Bernadine, and his sister Mary Ann run the restaurant. His other sister, Vitza, makes the famous chicken-*andouille* gumbo. And Bozo mans the stoves in the kitchen, frying wild catfish, oysters, and butterflied shrimp to pile on Leidenheimer's bread.

Crescent City Steak House

Franklin Delano Roosevelt won the 1932 election in part because he promised to end Prohibition. In 1933 New Orleans breweries celebrated repeal by giving away half a million gallons of beer. Huey Long, who tried to circumvent the thirteenth amendment legally by calling alcohol "medicine," sipped whiskey at his desk in the governor's mansion.

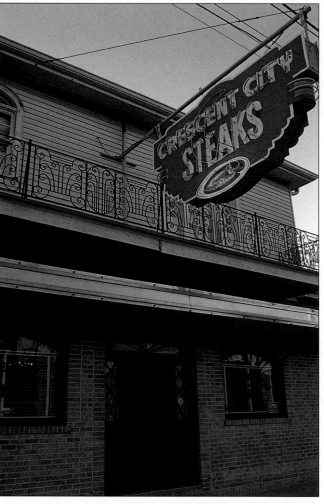

Yet another link in the New Orleans-Croatia connection, Crescent City Steak House, opened in 1934 in the same neighborhood as the old Bozo's. Here, John Vojkovich, from the Croatian island of Hvar, made culinary history by cooking steaks a new way—sizzling in butter. The tasty technique was copied by other local steak joints and, today, characterizes the way New Orleans does beef.

The building, designed as a bar and restaurant with a residence upstairs, dates to around 1913. The Vojkovich family lived above the business for thirty years.

Before the interstate system routed traffic around New Orleans in the sixties, Crescent City Steak House got a lot more travelers stopping for a roadside meal. Today their clients are loyal locals; some families have eaten here for four generations. An impressive list of the powerful and famous found their way to the unassuming little restaurant. Muhammad Ali, Earl Long, Carlos Marcello, Jim Garrison, and even Elvis put away a Crescent City steak.

Vojkovich's sons, Anthony and Frank, now run the business with their mother, Krasna. The family keeps this time capsule tightly sealed. The booths were already in place in 1949 when John Vojkovich expanded his one-room steakhouse, and nothing has changed since.

Except for Arnaud's private chambers with call buzzers for the waiters, Crescent City's booths may be the most secluded tables in town. Curtains provide the draped intimacy of a sheik's tent inside the wooden cubicles.

On the back walls of the booths hang scribbled orders taken by waiters in 1946 when a steak cost $1.30 and coffee was ten cents. One party had three salads, three steaks, two potatoes, three beers, and twenty-four drinks, all for $19.26.

INTO THE SWING ERA

By the 1930s the main ingredients in New Orleans' cultural court-bouillon were stewing all over the city. Dining establishments of every kind opened during the Great Depression, a century after cotton gave New Orleans its golden age of the 1830s and 1840s. FDR was president, and America was slowly being dragged into the conflict in Europe.

Mother's

Great cheap lunches have kept Mother's very busy for sixty-five years. In the twenty-first century, the recurring line out the door on Poydras Street testifies of Chef Jerry Amato's ability to put big piles of delicious on French bread for about five dollars.

It's called a po' boy because it's a lot of food for a little money, and economy was a chief concern when Simon Landry opened Mother's Restaurant in 1938.

Over the years, five members of the Landry family served in the marines, so hungry members of the corps joined a crew of longshoremen who were always faithful to Mother's.

In 1986, Landry's sons sold the operation to Jerry and John Amato. The Amato brothers have maintained Mother's unquestioned po'-boy supremacy and old-time cafeteria décor (or lack thereof). Memories hang from every inch of Mother's walls like the shredded cabbage and roast-beef debris spilling over the sides of gravy-soaked bread.

According to the guys at Mother's, in one year they go through 100,000 pounds each of ham and roast beef, 200,000 pounds of cabbage, 75,000 loaves of French bread, and 1,000 gallons of Creole mustard.

A year before Mother's opened, *Gone With the Wind* won the Pulitzer Prize and Amelia Earhart disappeared into the Pacific. The same year that Mother's opened, Orson Wells' *War of the Worlds* sent terrified listeners panicking into the streets.

Hansen's Sno-Bliz

Around the time Mr. Landry started serving po'-boy sandwiches to hungry dock workers on Poydras Street, Hansen's Sno-Bliz opened in Uptown, creating a delightful destination for summer-evening family strolls.

Flavored ice has pleased palates since ancient Oriental cultures combined syrups and snow. But in New Orleans in the twentieth century, flavored shaved ice reached new summits of veneration. The sweetest memories of all Uptown children drip with July snowballs soaked with strawberry, coconut, nectar, or chocolate syrup from the rainbow of bottles at Hansen's.

Ernest Hansen invented a motorized ice shaver in 1934 and the perfect snowball was born. He and his wife, Mary, still run the Tchoupitoulas Street business with their granddaughter Ashley. The Hansen Sno-Bliz machine shaves away behind a little curtain, insuring that the secret of the perfect snowball remains in the family.

Dooky Chase's

In 1941 Emily Chase moved her sandwich shop on Orleans Avenue across the street to open a tiny corner restaurant and bar where her husband, Edgar "Dooky" Chase, Sr., would also sell lottery tickets. People in the neighborhood started stopping by to play the lottery and were tempted to taste Emily's sausage po' boys. Slowly the shop grew into a fine Creole restaurant, a prized New Orleans institution, and an important social center of the African-American community.

Emily, a smart businesswoman, kept a cigar box full of money on Friday afternoons to cash paychecks for the neighborhood men. The men would stay for a beer or two, or sometimes all night. An oyster sandwich was the "peace-maker" they brought home to their angry wives.

Emily's son, also called Dooky, led a big band in the forties, when the boys came back from the war and America went wild for swing. The Dooky Chase Orchestra included great young musicians like Benny Powell, Emery Thompson, Vernel Fournier, Arnold DePass, and Warren Bell, Sr. These men went on to play with Louis Armstrong, Lionel Hampton, and Count Basie.

Dooky, the jazz-band leader, fell in love with and married an unlikely bride. Leah Lange, the oldest of eleven children, hated musicians and didn't like to cook. She became the matriarch of the restaurant and a legendary chef. Her daughter, also named Leah, is now a jazz singer.

During segregation, the restaurant played an important role as the only fine-dining establishment for African-Americans. Lena Horne, Sarah Vaughn, and the Jackson family ate here. White customers broke the law to meet at Dooky's with black friends, to have biracial business lunches, and maybe just to taste the chicken stuffed with oyster dressing and grillades in red sauce.

"In New Orleans, restaurants are more important than the food; they're political," says Leah, who has been creating dishes in Dooky's kitchen since 1954. She believes that solving the problems of the world today requires getting people back to the dinner table. She has gifted her neighborhood with etiquette and tradition, in addition to half a century of good food.

Today, the original 1941 location, a classic neighborhood saloon, is just a small section in the corner of Dooky Chase's restaurant, which has taken over the entire block, incorporating several old shotgun houses.

We are a bunch of weirdos down here all by ourselves. We don't eat Southern in New Orleans, no greens, no cornbread. They eat catfish and hush puppies as close as Baton Rouge. They are Southern. Soul food here is gumbo, jambalaya, and red beans and rice.

—Leah Chase

Leah's grandson is called Dooky Chase, like his father, grandfather, and great-grandfather.

Not long after Emily and Dooky Chase combined their endeavors in a shop selling sandwiches and lottery tickets, Franky Gaudin and Johnny Morreale took over an old riverfront bar called the Sunset Club and turned it into a seafood joint.

Gaudin and Morreale were double brothers-in-law—they each married the other's sister. Their restaurant has been one of New Orleans' favorites for sixty years.

The Morreale family still owns the building, but the business is leased to George Cortello, who runs Franky and Johnny's with his sons. Except for a recent invention, fried bell peppers, the menu has stayed the same, rich in crawfish pies and boiled shrimp.

More than just locals have discovered this low-slung, out-of-the-way eatery over the years: Cortello recently delivered a big tub of boiled crawfish to Air Force One.

PLEASE...
WAIT
TO BE
SEATED
BECK'S

Gumbo Shop

Artist Marc Anthony created the mural in the main dining room in 1925. The scene, painted on the burlap covers of cotton bales, depicts an early nineteenth-century military formation in Jackson Square when it was still the Place d'Armes, before the statue of Andrew Jackson was placed in the center of the gardens in 1856.

In one of the Vieux Carré's oldest buildings, one of the city's famous restaurants has been serving quintessential Creole food since 1945. The Gumbo Shop, founded by Margaret Popora, spreads throughout a 1795 Creole townhouse, its slave quarter, carriageway, and courtyard.

Merchant Pedro Commagere constructed the building, half a block from Jackson Square, to house a business on the first floor and residence above.

Mosca's

The trademark essences of a great Italian kitchen waft over a bleak stretch of marshland on Highway 90, forty-five minutes west of New Orleans. There's almost no other hint that a great culinary institution is nearby.

Johnny Mosca and Mary Mosca Marconi, members of the second generation of the family who gave New Orleans one of its greatest gourmet destinations, preside over a kitchen specializing in an altered state of consciousness brought on by garlic bliss.

Mosca's is a regional classic. It even has a plaque from the James Beard Foundation that says so. But New Orleans connoisseurs don't need anyone to tell them that this little white shack is a shrine of Sicilian Creole cuisine.

Provino and Lisa Mosca came to the United States from Sicily in the 1920s and opened restaurants in the Chicago Heights area. Two of their children drifted south. Mary married a New Orleans man in 1944, and Nicholas visited Louisiana after serving in the navy in World War II. Nick loved the area full of game, oysters, and alligators on the outskirts of the city. Soon, the parents followed and established Mosca's in 1946.

At the little shack near Avondale, Louisiana, the family created an amazing menu using central-Italian preparation and local ingredients. Nick then went on to become chef and co-owner of the Elmwood Plantation restaurant from 1962 to 1978. When the Elmwood restaurant burned down, he lent his talent to La Louisiane, Lenfant's, and the Fair Grounds before he retired his toque. Nick died in 1997.

Remember Antoine's world-famous oyster dish—"One of the great culinary creations of all time?" Well, sorry, Monsieur Alciatore, but New Orleans food critic Tom Fitzmorris says the Italian oysters Nick Mosca created with his father, baked in a mush of garlic, herbs, olive oil, and breadcrumbs, "is and always has been one of the two or three best oyster dishes in town, even surpassing the more famous Rockefeller."

But much of the Mosca magic is attributed to Mama Mosca, Lisa Angelotti Mosca, who devoted her life to every detail of the homemade ravioli, sausage, and slow-roasted chicken *à la grande.*

Nick Mosca's connection to Carlos Marcello has long been a source of Mafia-related speculation. They say Carlos Marcello had a private table in the kitchen in the 1970s and may have even provided the start-up funds for the little wood-frame home of Louisiana's best chicken cacciatore and crab salad. Whether it is true or not ceases to matter as you finish off the second or third mouthful of oyster rapture with a sip of crisp white wine from a short Italian-style glass.

Camellia Grill

The war was over. The baby boom was just getting started. Diners and drugstore fountains were all the rage in America.

In the Uptown neighborhood called Riverbend, where St. Charles Avenue ends at the Mississippi River levee, Camellia Grill opened on December 19, 1946, and still serves an old style of fast food with linen napkins, the way it was done during the Truman administration.

In the forties, a quality Camellia Grill hamburger with fresh-squeezed orange juice cost about thirty cents.

Twenty-nine stools fixed at a meandering bar provide a view of the fast-paced action behind the counter, where waiters in white uniforms pour eggs and flip burgers, nonstop. Six thousand eggs and a thousand pounds of hamburger meat hit the grills in an average week. Camellia's waiters, the Harlem Globetrotters of the short-order world, perform behind-the-back cheese tosses and fancy deliveries of drinking straws.

Camellia Grill competes with Antoine's in the loyal-staff category. Bat has been here fifty years, Harry comes in second at forty-eight years, and some of the newer guys have put in twelve years behind the counter. The customers are loyal, too. A few patrons have been coming for so many years that the Grill stopped charging them a long time ago.

Camellia Grill was the hobby of its founder, Jimmy Schwartz, Sr., who kept busy with other businesses. At the beginning, the Schwartz family made a progressive decision to hire black men as waiters and put them in the front, serving customers, while most restaurants in the city at the time kept black staff out of sight in the kitchen.

When the Grill moved in, the old house at 626 South Carrollton had been a double residence. Schwartz built the dining room and added the Greek columns in front. Since then, not much has changed.

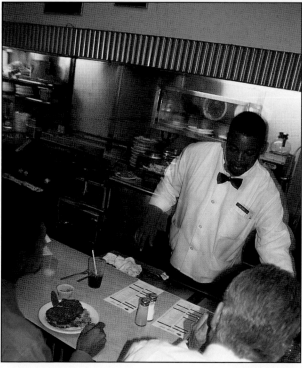

This Mid-City Italian Creole institution has Louis Prima on the jukebox, huge frozen mugs of Barq's root beer, fried pickles, and Frenchulettas. They have been passing spaghetti and fried seafood po' boys from the kitchen through a hole in the wall since at least 1947, about the same time that Prima, New Orleans' favorite Italian son, began to jump, jive, and wail his way to stardom.

A corner grocery owned by Michael T. Martin at Bienville and Telemachus streets became a grocery, restaurant, and bar in the 1940s. Martin ran the business with members of the Liuzza family. Sometime after World War II, the old grocery building was torn down and the new building called Liuzza's appeared.

Theresa Galbo started as a waitress at Liuzza's in 1957, and twenty-four years later, she bought the place. "Ms. T." decided to put a muffuletta on French bread instead of the round loaf because when she bought the traditional round bread just for muffulettas, it sometimes went to waste—*voilà!* the Frenchuletta. Galbo's son Michael mixed up a signature olive salad for the sandwich when he was just a child.

Today, Michael runs Liuzza's, keeping it much as it was in the swing era.

Brennan's Rex Room—Since 1872, the School of Design (better known as the Krewe of Rex) has had a secret membership of the city's most prominent leaders and businessmen. These wealthy New Orleans insiders know how to dine in style, and several of the city's great restaurants have dedicated a room to the royal krewe. Brennan's Rex Room is one of the most beautiful spaces in town.

THE BIRTH OF A DINING DYNASTY

Brennan's

In the 1950s, Brennan's restaurant moved to its current location, a historic mansion at 417 Royal Street. The home was built in 1794 for Vincent Rillieux, great-grandfather of Edgar Degas. From 1805 to 1820, it housed the Banque de la Louisiane, the first financial institution in the entire Louisiana Purchase territory.

In 1828 Andrew Jackson visited here when it was the home of Martin Gordon. But the house's most interesting resident must have been Paul Morphy, considered the top chess player in the world at age fifteen. Legend has it that 150 years ago, in what is now Brennan's Rex Room, the young Morphy played chess, using his servants as game pieces on a giant chessboard painted on the floor.

Here begins the unlikely story of New Orleans' greatest restaurant family. Owen Edward Brennan became a restaurateur in 1946 on a dare.

Brennan had managed the Court of Two Sisters for a short time and was a very popular proprietor at the Old Absinthe House, when his friend, Count Arnaud of Arnaud's restaurant, made a fateful remark. Arnaud, a haughty Frenchman, declared Irishmen fit to run hamburger joints but not fine restaurants. Brennan, a son of Irish immigrants, responded by opening Owen Brennan's French and Creole Restaurant (known as Brennan's Vieux Carré) and making it one of the finest establishments in town.

Over half a century later, the Brennans reign as the royal family of New Orleans' culinary kingdom, with eight prominent restaurants (not including those in other cities) and a gourmet grocery.

Owen started Brennan's famous breakfast after the success of a novel featuring another New Orleans restaurant. *Dinner at Antoine's*, Frances Parkinson Keyes' murder mystery about the city's hot-blooded high society, came out in 1948. Breakfast at Brennan's would be Owen's version of the glamorous restaurant life depicted in the book. A feast of eggs Benedict, eggs Hussarde, grillades and grits, crabmeat omelets, and more, washed down with champagne, Bloody Marys, brandy milk punch, and dark New Orleans coffee, became a Sunday-morning meal *de rigueur* and has remained so for generations.

The breakfast tradition inspired the restaurant's rooster logo.

The Rex Room overlooks Royal Street, and twelve formal dining rooms surround Brennan's courtyard, where iron tables on ancient flagstones sit among magnolias and elephant ears.

The famously charming and much-loved "Happy Irishman" Owen Brennan died in his sleep in 1955. His last night was surely a happy one: a prestigious wine-club dinner at Antoine's.

Owen's young sister, Ella, who had worked with him at the Vieux Carré on Bourbon Street, took over at Brennan's.

In 1969, Ella and the other siblings purchased Commander's Palace in the Garden District.

A falling-out among family members in the 1970s left Brennan's restaurant in the hands of Owen's three sons and Commander's controlled by his siblings. Today Owen's sons and grandsons carry on the odd family legacy at one of New Orleans' finest restaurants—the great French Creole institution built by a plucky Irishman.

The old slave quarter of the Rillieux mansion now holds Brennan's 35,000 bottles. The wine collection is so extensive that they run it like a separate business, with three employees devoted solely to oenological operations.

Brennan's does a magnificent version of the New Orleans drink that started the gourmet-coffee craze. Café Brulot (invented at Antoine's in the mid-1800s) is a presentation as much as a libation. The waiter peels an orange in a continuous piece and ladles a bowl of flaming Grand Marnier, Cognac, and brandy so that it spirals down the orange peel. The blue flames are doused with coffee and the whole magic mixture, including cloves, cinnamon, and sugar, is strained into *demitasse* cups.

Breakfast, lunch, and dinner, Brennan's most requested item is another flaming specialty, Bananas Foster with ice cream and warm rum sauce. In the 1950s, Owen charged Chef Paul Blangé with creating a fine dish with one of New Orleans' top imports. They named it for Owen's good friend and loyal Brennan's customer, Richard Foster.

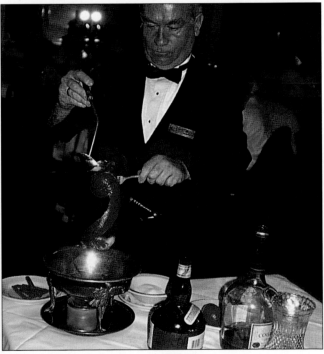

Owen Edward Brennan, founder of Brennan's restaurant, had five siblings: Ella, Richard, Dottie, John, and Adelaide. The five became known as "the Commander's Palace Brennans" after purchasing Commander's in 1969. This branch of the Brennan family went on to open Mr. B's Bistro, Bacco, Red Fish Grill, the Palace Café, Dickie Brennan's Steakhouse, and Foodies Kitchen, as well as other restaurants outside New Orleans.

Mr. B's Bistro

In 1979 Ralph and Cindy Brennan brought something remarkably fresh to the table at New Orleans' two-century-old dinner party. Before Mr. B's opened on Royal Street, formal dining was black tie and casual dining was po' boys. New Orleans' first gourmet bistro served fine cuisine in a relaxed atmosphere and started an ongoing trend.

Mr. B was the nickname of Ralph and Cindy's grandfather, who emigrated from Ireland, Owen Patrick Brennan, father of Brennan's founder, Owen Edward.

Paul Prudhomme headed the kitchen in Mr. B's early years. Following Prudhomme, the Brennans staffed Mr. B's kitchen with two chefs, a step that would allow them to bridge a culinary gap and stay on the cutting edge of Creole. Jimmy Smith came in from Brennan's to put the old Creole tradition on the stove, and Gerard Maras from Commander's brought a few skillets full of New American-style cuisine.

Mr. B's was the first in New Orleans to feature a wood-burning grill and made a big splash with redfish cooked over hickory. Pasta dishes with Creole flavor had not been on New Orleans menus before pasta jambalaya and other Italian Creole innovations emerged from Mr. B's kitchen.

Two later establishments would branch out on the Brennan family tree with Mr. B's originals as their inspiration. Bacco does fine Italian Creole, and the Red Fish Grill does exactly what its name implies.

Bacco

Bacco is Italian for the Latin *Bacchus,* the mythical god of wine and merriment. Ralph and Cindy Brennan, of the Commander's Palace branch of the Brennan family, introduced this deity in 1991.

Twelve years after Mr. B's introduced pasta jambalaya to New Orleans, Bacco elaborated on the theme of gourmet Italian-New Orleans fare. Bacco does Italian Creole the way Antoine Alciatore cooked French Creole, adapting Old World recipes to Louisiana ingredients, with results like crawfish ravioli and crabmeat lasagna.

The setting, like the food, is a Mediterranean-New Orleans mix that would please the joyful vine god. In a mid-nineteenth-century building on Chartres Street, modern Italian lines blend with old French Quarter brick walls and Fortuni chandeliers. Where the old courtyard used to be sits Bacco's main dining room, lit by skylights in a magnificent vaulted ceiling.

Red Fish Grill

Ralph Brennan has a history with grilled redfish that started at Mr. B's twenty years ago. To house his newest venture, inspired by swimming things and flaming hickory, Brennan converted a corner of the old D. H. Holmes department store into an artistic, contemporary space, with sea creatures etched into the ocean-colored concrete floor and swimming in neon overhead.

Red Fish Grill serves Gulf shellfish, finfish, alligator sausage, and raw oysters on tables painted by local artist Luis Colmenares. Colmenares also sculpted the palms branching off the iron support columns and the giant oyster-shell mirrors above the bar.

When D. H. Holmes expanded and took over this section of Bourbon Street in the 1860s, the department store converted several older townhouses into its men's department. Almost a century and a half later, while building Red Fish Grill, Ralph Brennan decided to preserve the crumbling antebellum walls and incorporate them into the restaurant's design.

One of the old walls separates the bar from the dining room. Old black-and-white photographs of Louisiana's bayous cover the wall. Ralph Brennan's mother, Claire, took the pictures in 1948 as part of her photography thesis at Newcomb College.

Palace Café

Dickie Brennan, a second-generation Commander's Palace Brennan, opened a new Palace in 1991. And following in the footsteps of its paternal progenitor, the Palace Café quickly amassed a long list of awards saturated with superlatives.

The Parisian-style grand café occupies the old Werlein's music store, a century-old Beaux Arts landmark on Canal Street. America's oldest music company, Werlein's dates back to 1842. After operating the Canal Street location from 1852 to 1990, the music store moved its downtown operation to the 200 block of Decatur Street. The names of Werlein's old departments—Guitars, Organs, Pianos, and Sheet Music—still light up above the door in the Palace Café elevator.

A mural, painted by Marilyn Carter Rougelot portraying New Orleans jazz musicians, surrounds the upper floor of the grand space created by architect Stewart Farnet and designer Mark Knauer.

Creole and Cajun delights flow from the kitchen, along with some unexpected originals like crabmeat cheesecake, oyster pan roast, and white-chocolate bread pudding.

1ST GUITARS
BAND SHEET MUSIC
PRO KEYBOARDS

2ND ORGANS
PIANOS
STUDIOS

3RD
BAND REPAIR

4TH CASHIER
CREDIT OFFICE
OFFICES

FIFTIES AND SIXTIES

Before we take a giant leap into the later decades of the twentieth century, here are a few more of New Orleans' beloved institutions that opened before Elvis was the king and before *Apollo 11* reached the moon.

Venezia

Venezia is the Italian name for Venice, although the food at this old Mid-City haunt has a more southern-Italian flavor. For forty-five years, locals have slurped spaghetti and meatballs in this turn-of-the-century storehouse before heading a block down to Brocato's for Italian ice and cannoli. Some of the waiters have been around for more than twenty years, serving eggplant Vatican to third- and fourth-generation customers.

Added to the taste of Venezia's classic red sauce and veal parmigiana is the spicy history of its connection to the mob. Anthony Carollo, identified by federal investigators as the godfather of the New Orleans crime family, founded the restaurant and ran it for twenty years. Carollo's father had been the local Mafia boss prior to the era of the infamous Carlos Marcello.

Rocky and Carlo's

Like Mosca's near Avondale, Rocky and Carlo's is a suburban Sicilian institution with a devoted, maybe even addicted, New Orleans following. Natives will drive a long way for a plate of Rocky and Carlo's baked macaroni.

In Chalmette, less than a mile from the battlefield where Andrew Jackson's troops whipped the British at the Battle of New Orleans, Rocky and Carlo's serves as an important social and political center with serious garlic bread and decadent fried seafood.

Like Franky and Johnny of the famous Uptown boiled-crawfish establishment, Rocky and Carlo were brothers-in-law twice over. Childhood friends who married each other's sisters, Rocky Tommaseo and Cologero "Carlo" Gioe came to Louisiana from Sicily, and together with their brothers, Guisseppi Gioe, Tommy Tommaseo, and Mario Gioe, opened Rocky and Carlo's restaurant in 1965.

After almost half a century, Rocky, now in his eighties, sits at the cash register. He still goes in at two in the morning to make macaroni, and he still has a thick Italian accent. Carlo died recently after thirty years of daily devotion to the business.

Many unofficial St. Bernard Parish political meetings take place in Rocky and Carlo's Sicilian Room. "Sometimes people just want to eat in there," says Rocky. He usually lets them, after the typical Mediterranean ritual of cheerful wrangling over whether he will charge them extra.

Rib Room

The City Exchange Hotel, also called the Saint Louis, opened in 1838. The $1.5 million celebration of Creole luxury and river wealth amazed all who saw it, with a rotunda eighty-eight feet high, ornate ballrooms, dining salons, and accommodations for 600 guests.

In the years before the Civil War, music filled the ballrooms and the shouts of auctioneers lauded the strong backs of thousands of slaves. According to legend, at this hotel, a Spanish cook named Alvarez invented gumbo by thickening fish soup with okra.

The celebrating stopped with the Civil War. Then in 1874, in the waning days of Reconstruction, the Louisiana legislature purchased the old Saint Louis Hotel to house government offices. In 1882, when the state capitol moved to Baton Rouge, the Hotel Royal moved in. But the new hotel failed and the once-great building decayed, until it was finally torn down in 1916.

In 1960 a new large-scale hotel opened in the 600 block of St. Louis Street. The Royal Orleans (now the Omni Royal Orleans) resurrected the tradition of elegant accommodation and fine dining that had been snuffed out on the site a century before. But the new hotel's premier restaurant was surprisingly not Creole. Instead of competing with Antoine's and Brennan's, both within half a block, the hotel chose to model its Rib Room after an English steak house. A great rotisserie dominates the back wall. But a little local flavor shows up in the room: old railroad headlights hang from exposed brick columns marked with place names of rural Louisiana.

Archie Casbarian, the elegant Egyptian who would later resurrect Arnaud's restaurant, managed the Royal Orleans in the 1970s. Casbarian introduced the concept of food festivals to the hotel restaurant, the first being a Mexican fiesta with an imported mariachi band. Another of Casbarian's famous inspirations, a cart dispensing oversized martinis in chilled glasses, still rolls through the Rib Room.

Jacques-Imo's

Two of New Orleans' great Creole-soul restaurants sprang from seeds planted in the 1960s.

Austin Leslie became famous cooking at a restaurant on North Robertson Street founded by his aunt, Helene Dejean Pollock, in 1964. At Chez Heléne, they did everything from red beans to oysters Rockefeller the way God intended.

The *Underground Gourmet* named Chez Heléne number one in New Orleans in 1971, and after that, Chef Leslie didn't get much rest. In countless publications, Chez Heléne was lauded alongside the city's greats—Antoine's, Commander's, and Brennan's. It even inspired a television series called *Frank's Place* in the 1980s.

In 1996 Leslie found the perfect new showcase for his fabulous Creole-soul entrées when Jacques Leonardi, a chef trained at K-Paul's, opened a restaurant in the Carrollton area of Uptown, the old Café Savanna. At Jacques Imo's, the two cook up some serious New Orleans cuisine in a funky voodoo shotgun house.

Jacques-Imo's is a play on the owner's name and the word "jokamo," from a traditional Mardi Gras Indian call. Mardi Gras Indians trace their history to the mid-nineteenth century. Groups of black men adopted certain cultural elements of Native Americans, recalling times during slavery when rural Indians sheltered runaway slaves and shared a common struggle against the Europeans.

Distinctive rituals grew out of this strange bond, and at Carnival, black "chiefs" emerge and stroll through the streets in elaborate feathered and beaded costumes, accompanied by an entourage beating tambourines and singing the customary calls.

"Jokamo feena nay" is a Creole patois warning to someone who might challenge your chief, telling him to get out of the way. Singer/pianist Dr. John recorded a hit song from the Indian call and defines jokamo as a mocker or joker. Sugarboy Crawford, the Dixie Cups, and the Neville Brothers also recorded musical versions of this infectious back-street New Orleans exclamation.

Zachary's

Less than a block from Jacques-Imo's, the Baquet family continues a tradition of great Creole soul food started by Eddie Baquet, Sr., thirty-five years ago in New Orleans' Seventh Ward. Eddie's restaurant, source of amazing home-cooked gumbo, pork chops, and seafood, remained a local secret until Bill Cosby fell in love with the place and waxed rhapsodic about Eddie's fried chicken on the *Tonight Show*.

The original Eddie's closed in 1999, and Eddie's son, Wayne Baquet, opened a new restaurant on Oak Street named for his own son.

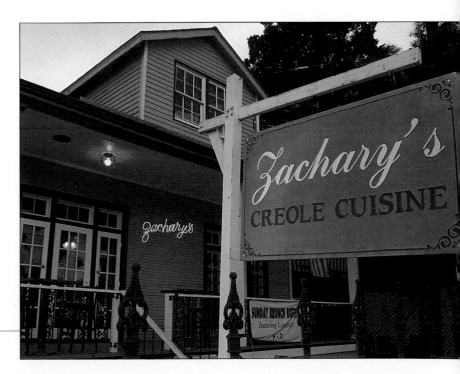

CREOLE IN THE LAST THIRTY YEARS

In the last three decades, New Orleans' great dinner party spread around the globe. Chef Emeril, the Jules Alciatore of the twenty-first century, now fires up the enthusiasm of culinary fanatics across multiple time zones several times a day. Susan Spicer, the modern Madame Begue, cannot stop winning international awards for blending dollops of Asia, the Mediterranean, and Provence into a new style of Creole. New Orleans-themed restaurants operate everywhere from Seattle to Sydney.

K-Paul's Louisiana Kitchen

After heating up the kitchen at Commander's Palace and Mr. B's, Chef Paul Prudhomme opened his famous French Quarter spot in 1979 and named it for his wife, Kay, and himself. Here, Prudhomme reached unprecedented culinary stardom by searing fish into dark-crusted juiciness and firing up creative versions of spicy Cajun classics. Soon, Cajun menus appeared around the planet.

Prudhomme stoked up diners' desire for redfish almost to the point of extinction. Laws to prevent over-fishing were passed in 1988, and a whole new industry hatched. Today, only farm-raised redfish appear on New Orleans' restaurant platters.

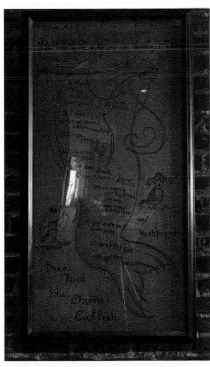

Drawings by Sally Lincks Sunseri, depicting Cajun recipes, decorate K-Paul's walls.

Brigtsen's

Frank Brigtsen was a student of Paul Prudhomme and started his cooking career under the famous chef at Commander's Palace. He then followed Prudhomme to K-Paul's.

In 1986, with funding from his mentor, Brigtsen and his wife, Marna, bought the old Dante by the River in the Riverbend area Uptown. In the converted Victorian shotgun house, Brigtsen took the colorful palette of blackened Cajun, fine Creole, and New American that was New Orleans cuisine in the 1980s and created his own original series of masterpieces.

Gabrielle

A culinary romance heated up over the skillets at K-Paul's kitchen in 1984, when a young line cook named Mary Blanchard met Greg Sonnier, the new sausage maker. By the time Greg had been promoted to line cook and Mary was dessert chef, they were headed for a blackened Cajun wedding.

Greg's career took him to the Windsor Court and then to work with fellow Prudhomme protégé Frank Brigtsen in 1986.

In 1992 Greg and Mary gave birth to a bouncing baby restaurant on Esplanade Avenue in the wedge-shaped building that had formerly been Mystery Street Café. They named the place after their real daughter, Gabrielle, and all New Orleans became a part of the family celebration.

In 1994 *Food and Wine* magazine named Greg one of the top ten young chefs in America for his tasty creations, like barbecue-shrimp pie, cracker-crusted rabbit, and crawfish enchilada.

Gamay is the latest fruit of the Sonniers' love match, named for the wine grape variety that closely resembles the blend of the couple's first names. The French Quarter establishment features fine wines and Continental cuisine but doesn't leave out the fried chicken and red beans and rice.

Peristyle

The corner building at North Rampart and Dumaine streets, on the edge of the French Quarter, retains tangible links to its culinary past—a century of inspired dining. The old front steps are tiled with the name "Gentilich," an upscale oyster and seafood restaurant that operated in the building long ago. Murals of City Park, painted by Ferdinand Martin sometime before 1920, decorate the dining room, and an old terrazzo floor conspires with the dark wood of an antique bar to re-create an aura of old New Orleans.

In 1972 Marti's restaurant inherited the historic space and gave it another fine-dining era. The property next played muse to Chef John Neal, who came to the site in 1992 and raised the bar for the region's gourmet restaurants when he opened Peristyle, named for a landscape of the City Park peristyle mounted behind the bar.

The current owner-chef, Anne Kearney Sand, studied with Emeril Lagasse and was a sous-chef under John Neal. She bought Peristyle after Neal's death in 1995 and continued the legacy, quickly collecting shelves full of national awards.

BIBLIOGRAPHY

Arthur, Stanley Clisby. *Old New Orleans: Walking Tours of the French Quarter*. 1936. Reprint. Gretna, LA: Pelican Publishing Company, 1990.

Brennan, Pip, Jimmy Brennan, and Ted Brennan. *Breakfast at Brennan's and Dinner Too*. 2nd ed. New Orleans: Brennan's, Inc., 1994.

Bultman, Bethany Ewald. *New Orleans, Compass American Guide*. 4th ed. Oakland: Random House, 2000.

Cable, George Washington. *Old Creole Days*. 1879. Reprint. Gretna, LA: Pelican Publishing Company, 1991.

Cable, Mary. *Lost New Orleans*. Boston: Houghton Mifflin Company, 1980.

Chase, John Churchill. *Frenchmen, Desire, Good Children And Other Streets of New Orleans*. 1949. Reprint. Gretna, LA: Pelican Publishing Company, 2001.

Chase, Leah. *The Dooky Chase Cookbook*. Gretna, LA: Pelican Publishing Company, 1990.

DeMers, John. *French Quarter Royalty, The Tumultuous Life and Times of the Omni Royal Orleans*. New Orleans: Omni Royal Orleans, 1993.

_____ , and Geoff Kalish. *The Best Wining and Dining in New Orleans*. Fort Lee, NJ: The Best Wining and Dining in New Orleans/HCC, 1994.

Arnaud's Bacchus Room—Jane Casbarian commissioned George Dureau to create a portrait of the wine god to inspire revelry in one of Arnaud's small private rooms.

Dennery, Phyllis. *Dining In—New Orleans Cookbook*. Seattle: Peanut Butter Publishing, 1985.

Federal Writers' Project Guide to 1930s New Orleans, The. *The WPA Guide to New Orleans*. Historic New Orleans Collection ed. New York: Random House, 1983.

Folse, John. *The Evolution of Cajun & Creole Cuisine*. Brandon, MS: Quail Ridge Press, 1990.

_____. *Hot Beignets & Warm Boudoirs*. Gonzales, LA: Chef John D. Folse & Co., 1999.

Huber, Leonard V. *New Orleans: A Pictorial History*. Gretna, LA: Pelican Publishing Company, 1991.

Laborde, Peggy Scott. Introduction to *Gumbo Shop, A New Orleans Restaurant Cookbook,* by Richard Stewart. New Orleans: Gumbo Shop, 1999.

_____. *Lost Restaurants of New Orleans*. New Orleans: WYES TV, Greater New Orleans Educational Television Foundation, 2001.

Lawson, Lewis. "Pilgrim in the City: Walker Percy." In *Literary New Orleans*, edited by Richard S. Kennedy. Baton Rouge, LA: LSU Press, 1998.

Mariani, John. *America Eats Out*. New York: William Morrow and Company, 1991.

Naylor, Honey. *The Insider's Guide to New Orleans*. Boston: The Harvard Common Press, 1994.

Preuss, Gunter, and Evelyn Preuss. *Broussard''s Restaurant Cookbook*. Gretna, LA: Pelican Publishing Company, 1996.

Skolnik, Rayna. *Great Restaurants of the World, Commander's Palace*. New York: Lebhar-Friedman Books, 2000.

Stanforth, Deirdre. *The New Orleans Restaurant Cookbook*. Garden City, NJ: Doubleday and Company, 1967.

Brennan's Red Room on the second floor of the historic Rillieux mansion, also known as the Paul Morphy house

INDEX

Acme Oyster House, 724 Iberville, 522-5973, 60-61

Andrea's, 3100 Nineteenth, Metairie, 834-8583, 185

Antoine's, 713 St. Louis, 581-4422, 18-29

Arnaud's, 813 Bienville, 523-5433, 62-71

Bacco, 310 Chartres, 522-2426, 142-43

Bayona, 430 Dauphine, 525-4455, 164-65

Bistro at Maison de Ville, The, 733 Toulouse, 528-9206, 162-63

Bozo's, 3117 Twenty-First, Metairie, 831-8666, 108-9

Brennan's, 417 Royal, 525-9711, 132-39

Brigtsen's, 723 Dante, 861-7610, 158

Brocato's, 214 North Carrollton, 486-0078, 82-83

Broussard's, 819 Conti, 581-3866, 72-76

Bruning's, 1922 West End, 282-9395, 36-37

Café Degas, 3127 Esplanade, 945-5635, 180

Café Du Monde Coffee Stand, 813 Decatur, 581-2914, 38-39

Café Sbisa, 1011 Decatur, 522-5565, 52-55

Camellia Grill, 626 South Carrollton, 866-9573, 128-29

Casamento's, 4330 Magazine, 895-9761, 92-93

Central Grocery, 923 Decatur, 523-1620, 84-85

Charlie's Steak House, 4510 Dryades, 895-9323, 98

Christian's, 3835 Iberville, 482-4924, 170-71

Clancy's, 6100 Annunciation, 895-1111, 176-79

Commander's Palace, 1403 Washington, 899-8221, 42-47

Court of Two Sisters, The, 613 Royal, 522-7261, 77-81

Crescent City Steak House, 101 North Broad, 821-3271, 110-11

Deanie's, 1713 Lake, Metairie, 831-4141, 153

Domilise, 5240 Annunciation, 899-9126, 94-95

Dooky Chase's, 2301 Orleans, 821-0600, 114-17

Emeril's, 800 Tchoupitoulas, 528-9393, 160

Emeril's Delmonico, 1300 St. Charles, 525-4937, 48-51

Feelings Cafe, 2600 Chartres, 945-2222, 172

Fiorella's, 1136 Decatur, 528-9566, 86-87

Franky and Johnny's, 321 Arabella, 899-9146, 118-21

Gabrielle, 3201 Esplanade, 948-6233, 159

Galatoire's, 209 Bourbon, 525-2021, 56-59

Gautreau's, 1728 Soniat, 899-7397, 174-75

Grill Room, (Windsor Court) 300 Gravier, 522-1992, 184

Gumbo Shop, 630 St. Peter, 525-1486, 122-23

Hansen's Sno-Bliz, 4801 Tchoupitoulas, 891-9788, 113

Irene's Cuisine , 539 St. Philip, 529-8811, 186

Jack Dempsey's, 738 Poland, 943-9914, 173

Jacques-Imo's, 8324 Oak, 861-0886, 154-55

Kim Son, 349 Whitney, Gretna, 366-2489, 188

K-Paul's, 416 Chartres, 524-7394, 156-57

La Crêpe Nanou, 1410 Robert, 899-2670, 180-81

Liuzza's Lounge and Grill, 1518 North Lopez, 943-8667, 99

Liuzza's Restaurant and Bar, 3636 Bienville, 482-9120, 130-31

Mandich, 3200 St. Claude, 947-9553, 101-3

Mandina's, 3800 Canal, 482-9179, 96-97

Morning Call Coffee Stand, 3325 Severn, Metairie, 885-4068, 40-41

Mosca's, 4137 U.S. Hwy 90 W, 436-9942, 124-27

Mother's, 401 Poydras, 523-9656, 112

Mr. B's, 201 Royal, 523-2078, 140-41

Napoleon House, 500 Chartres, 524-9752, 85

NOLA, 534 St. Louis, 522-6652, 161

Palace Café, 605 Canal, 521-1661, 146-47

Pascal's Manale, 1838 Napoleon, 895-4877, 88-91

Peristyle, 1041 Dumaine, 593-9535, 166-69

R & O's, 216 Hammond Hwy, Metairie, 831-1248, 153

Red Fish Grill, 115 Bourbon, 598-1200, 144-45

Red Room, 2040 St. Charles, 528-9759, 13

Rib Room, 621 St Louis, 529-7045, 150-51

Rocky and Carlo's, 613 West St. Bernard Hwy, Chalmette, 279-8323, 149

Ruth's Chris Steak House, 711 North Broad, 486-0810, 106-7

Sid-Mar's, 1824 Orpheum, Metairie, 831-9541, 152

Taqueria Corona, 5932 Magazine, 897-3974, 189

Tony Angello's, 6262 Fleur de Lis, 488-0888, 186-87

Tujague's, 823 Decatur, 525-8676, 30-35

Uglesich's, 1238 Baronne, 523-8571, 104-5

Upperline, 1413 Upperline, 891-9822, 182-83

Venezia, 134 N. Carrollton, 488-7991, 148

Zachary's, 8400 Oak, 865-155, 155

Note: All area codes are (504).